RICOEUR ON TIME AND NARRATIVE

RICOEUR ON TIME AND NARRATIVE

An Introduction to
Temps et récit

WILLIAM C. DOWLING

University of Notre Dame Press
Notre Dame, Indiana

Library of Congress Cataloging-in-Publication Data

Dowling, William C.
  Ricoeur on time and narrative : an introduction to Temps et récit / William
Dowling.
     p. cm.
  Includes bibliographical references and index.
  ISBN-13: 978-0-268-02608-0 (pbk. : alk. paper)
  ISBN-10: 0-268-02608-4 (pbk. : alk. paper)
  1. Ricœur, Paul. Temps et récit. 2. Mimesis in literature. 3. Time in literature.
4. Narration (Rhetoric) 5. Plots (Drama, novel, etc.) I. Title.
  PN212.R5236   2011
  809'.923—dc23

                        2011025674

♻ This book is printed on recycled paper.

For Myra Jehlen

CONTENTS

PREFACE

THE OBJECT OF THIS BOOK IS TO MAKE THE KEY CONCEPTS OF Paul Ricoeur's *Time and Narrative* available to readers who might have felt bewildered by the twists and turns of its argument. Those who don't read French may have assumed that their confusion was due to reading Ricoeur in translation. It is a reasonable enough assumption. What can be captured only approximately in another language might, after all, be luminously clear in the original. But that is not the case here. The English translation of *Temps et récit* is for the most part admirably reliable, and the experience of reading Ricoeur in English is pretty much the same as reading him in French. Indeed, existing commentary on Ricoeur shows that French readers have had their own difficulties with what can sometimes seem to be a perversely inconclusive style of philosophical argument. For readers new to Ricoeur, that style constitutes a major problem.

As François Dosse has shown in *Paul Ricoeur: Les sens d'une vie*, Ricoeur's style was shaped by his resistance to an opposite style of Paris philosophizing. In France this sometimes goes under the name of *parisianism*: the habit of treating argument as mere assertion and counter-assertion, along with a certain grandiosity of claims pushed to fantastic extremes. Dosse's account brings out, for instance, the full bitterness of the famous episode in which disciples of Jacques Lacan accused Ricoeur of having stolen Lacan's ideas for his own book on Freud. But behind that bitterness may be glimpsed a more abstract conflict of intellectual styles. One of these styles is represented by Lacan himself, a flamboyant public figure issuing to packed seminars a stream of gnomic pronouncements offered as a new theory of the Freudian unconscious. The other is represented by Ricoeur, working alone in his study, trying to isolate through endlessly patient analysis the implications of Freud's own theory of the unconscious for a philosophy of will and volition.

On the other hand, it is not immediately clear why analysis, no matter how painstaking, should count as argument. In 1970, Ricoeur was instrumental in introducing J. L. Austin's *How to Do Things with Words* to French readers. The title of the French translation, which has the virtue of at least hinting at such now-familiar concepts as performatives and constatives and illocutionary force, was *Quand dire, c'est faire.* But those who attended the original lectures on which Austin based *How to Do Things with Words* had no such guidance. Reading Ricoeur can sometimes seem like the experience they reported, a feeling of having somehow been set adrift on a sea of endless analysis that has no object but to lead to further analysis and then to still more. Nonetheless, as Austin saw, there comes a point at which analysis, if it is rigorous and purposeful enough, begins to show—cannot help but show—what it is all about. The same is true, with one important difference, of Ricoeur.

The difference is this. For Austin, the point of careful analysis was to bring to light truths not directly expressible in propositional terms. For Ricoeur, it is to push analysis to the point where there stands revealed, just beyond the limits of purely logical or rational argument, a lurking aporia or irresolvable paradox. The inescapability of such paradox serves as a guiding principle in Ricoeur's philosophy. For what the long history of philosophical investigation shows, he thinks, is that the deepest paradoxes of human experience—the paradox, for instance, of a rational consciousness able to contemplate its own existence but unable then to say what is doing the contemplating—cannot be resolved by philosophical argument. Neither, however, can they be avoided, at least so long as existence itself insistently keeps thrusting them in various disturbing guises upon our attention. The value of philosophy lies, in Ricoeur's view, in its perpetual struggle toward a goal of sense or meaning. Its danger lies in the temptation to believe that any truth one has managed to discover is absolute.

Ricoeur's usual method is to dismantle established theories and philosophical arguments until he is able to show that, no matter how great their contribution to understanding an important problem—the nature of mimetic representation, say, or the concept of causality in psychological as opposed to physical explanation—they have left some crucial issue unresolved. Even for those highly sympathetic to Ricoeur's approach, this process can sometimes seem to be too much an end in itself. Thus, for instance, we hear François Wahl—Ricoeur's longtime editor, and one of his most informed and perceptive readers—trying gently in 1984 to get Ricoeur to see that the second volume of *Temps et récit*, which Wahl has just finished reading in manuscript, far too often loses sight of its main object while straying off into incidental matters ("les annonces, les rappels, les expositions parfois accessoires.").[1] It is a note of frustration one comes across in Wahl's editorial correspondence with Ricoeur again and again over the years.

In hopes of sparing the reader that sort of frustration, I have chosen to write this book from a perspective I hit upon in discussions with Paul Ricoeur some years ago at an institute for advanced studies in the humanities. He and I occupied neighboring offices. Ricoeur was then in the early stages of writing *Time and Narrative*, and was concentrating on the work of Northrop Frye and Hayden White. My own background was in analytic philosophy. I knew, at that point, very little about French philosophy, but I did know a good bit about Northrop Frye and the formalist theory of W. K. Wimsatt and Monroe Beardsley at Yale and Reuben Brower and his students at Harvard, in which Ricoeur also took a keen interest. We had daily discussions, and subsequently wound up co-directing a fellows' seminar on the theory of literary autonomy, a subject that would greatly preoccupy Ricoeur in *Time and Narrative*. I also began, on my own, to read Ricoeur's previously published works.

For anyone used to the straightforward arguments of analytic philosophy, I found, the best way to see what Ricoeur was doing was to ignore the occasional glimpses of aporia or paradox in the remote distance and pay close attention instead to the way established theories and arguments were dissolving and reconstituting themselves under the pressure of his analysis. A great deal of Ricoeur's originality as a philosopher, normally unremarked in commentary on his work, seems to me to lie precisely in his power to sustain this sense of constant renewal. In *Time and Narrative*, as I shall try to show, there is real intellectual excitement involved in watching how such theories and arguments—Aristotle and Augustine and Husserl on time, Frye and A. J. Greimas on narrative structure, Arthur Danto and Louis O. Mink on the nature of historical explanation—emerge from Ricoeur's analysis not only transformed in themselves but in an entirely new set of relations to one another.

Commentary on Ricoeur has concentrated almost exclusively on what might be called the negative strain in his philosophy: the steady emphasis on a paradoxicality that denies all claims to absolute truth, or what in France is often celebrated as Ricoeur's own *renoncement au savoir absolu*. But there is also a strongly positive strain in Ricoeur's thinking, though it is admittedly harder to see, especially for first-time readers. My own breakthrough in understanding Ricoeur came when I realized that the strikingly original observations he kept coming up with while discussing the work of others were not mere random insights but related points in an extended argument that, though presented unsystematically, was meant to be understood in systematic terms. That is the line I have followed in *Ricoeur on Time and Narrative*. The subsequent chapters are devoted to reconstructing, from its dispersed presentation in three volumes of wide-ranging speculation on a variety of issues, what I take to be the underlying argument of *Temps et récit*. It perhaps goes without saying that I hope they might also suggest a useful way of understanding Ricoeur's work as a whole.

AS AN APPENDIX TO THE PRESENT WORK, I HAVE INCLUDED A SHORTENED version of an interview with Paul Ricoeur, originally published in *Magazine littéraire*. My translation first appeared in *Providence Studies in Western Civilization* 8, no. 2 (Fall/Winter 2004). I am grateful to the editors for granting permission to reprint this shorter version. In addition, I want to mention a number of personal debts. At the National Humanities Center, besides conversations with Paul Ricoeur, daily discussions with David Falk greatly aided my grasp of issues addressed in the following chapters. Subsequently, a number of people—Linda Dowling, Kit Fine, Russell Goodman, Ruth Marcus, G. F. Schueler, the late Jerrold

Katz—have made similar contributions in discussions regular or occasional. Earlier versions of the manuscript were read by Thomas Pavel and Michael Wood. Both made suggestions that led to greater precision at crucial points in my exegesis. I am grateful to them both. At the University of Notre Dame Press, Rebecca DeBoer's splendidly attentive editorial work saved me from several outright errors and very many stylistic infelicities. At Rutgers, *Ricoeur on Time and Narrative* owes an important debt to the lively and skeptical intelligence of the students in English 491, a special undergraduate seminar on narratology held in Bishop House in the fall semester of 2010. Its debt to Myra Jehlen, whose extraordinary *Five Fictions in Search of Truth* inspired that seminar, and who, at an extremely busy period in her life, let herself be talked into co-teaching it with me, is registered in the dedication to this volume.

Chapter One

MIMESIS

AT THE CENTER OF RICOEUR'S PHILOSOPHICAL ARGUMENT IN *Time and Narrative* lies an extended exercise in what looks like purely literary analysis, namely, his reconsideration—ultimately, as we shall see, his radical reinterpretation—of the concept of *mythos* or narrative emplotment in Aristotle's *Poetics*. Yet this, too, belongs to philosophy. As Ricoeur understands it, Aristotle's account of *mythos* was nothing less than an attempt to come to terms with what the Greeks called mimesis, a word sometimes translated as "imitation," sometimes as "representation," but always as something having to do with that puzzling intuition that makes us want to say that art imitates life. For Plato, whose notion of mimesis drew mainly on the visual arts—the way a portrait or a marble bust can be said to imitate its subject, say—the idea was relatively unproblematic. For Aristotle, who by the time he wrote the *Poetics* had begun to wonder exactly what a tragedy like *Oedipus Rex* or an epic like the *Iliad* could be said to be representing or imitating, it had assumed the status of a philosophical problem.

Aristotle's solution, famously, was to say that a work like *Oedipus Rex* is the imitation of an action. So long as we do not stray too far from Plato's notion of mimesis as a copy—Ricoeur says "redoubling"—of some original, the notion has a good deal of plausibility. I can, at any rate, imagine without undue strain a social event like a dinner party where, unknown to the guests, a recording of the conversation was being made. And I can then imagine a group of actors, provided with

1

a transcript, later reenacting that event. Yet this could not have been what Aristotle, whose notion of *poiēsis* was meant precisely to account for imaginative or fictional works, had in mind. This is no doubt why the problem of mimesis is clearest in works set in imaginary surroundings. In some obvious sense, Shakespeare's *Julius Caesar* can be seen as an imitation of actions that took place in history. But in what world and in what time—unless we want to say, risking outright tautology, in the world and time of the play itself—did the action imitated in *A Midsummer Night's Dream* take place?

This is not simply a problem about mimesis. *A Midsummer Night's Dream*, not least in its obvious proximity to a now vanished culture of folklore and magic, may be seen to raise in particularly insistent terms the problem of literary autonomy—the idea, which Ricoeur wholly endorses, that literary works are self-contained worlds with their own laws and their own logic, subject to distortion when made to answer to ideologies or doctrines external to themselves. At an inaugural moment in literary theory, this is part of what Aristotle had in mind in saying that poetry—by which, as I have noted, he meant imaginative writing generally—was a more philosophical and more universal thing than history. It is what Sidney would later mean in saying, in the *Apology for Poesy*, that art gives us a golden world and nature only a brazen one, and what is then distantly echoed in Shelley's notion of poets as the unacknowledged legislators of mankind. In *Time and Narrative*, it is precisely Ricoeur's controlling awareness of the claims of literary autonomy that moves him toward a vastly more complex understanding of Aristotle's *mimēsis praxeōs*, or "imitation of an action."

The best way to understand *mimēsis praxeōs*, Ricoeur believes, is to begin by freeing the concept of "imitation" from any narrowly conceived comparison of art work and object, as in the physical resemblance between a marble bust and its subject. What then comes to light is an alternative notion of *mythos* as what Ricoeur calls an arc of operations, a complex movement that originates in culture understood as a symbolic order, that then passes into fixed or frozen form in a work like the *Iliad* or *Don Quixote* or *Middlemarch*, and that is then finally reintroduced into the cultural sphere in the consciousness of listeners or readers whose way of being in the world has been altered by their reading. To these three sectors of the arc Ricoeur gives the names, respectively, of Mimesis$_1$, Mimesis$_2$, and Mimesis$_3$, a nomenclature that never becomes cumbersome so long as one remains aware that they are three stages or phases of what *Time and Narrative* treats throughout as a single continuous process.

At the level of Mimesis$_1$, to which he variously refers as the prenarrative structure of experience, a prenarrative level of understanding, or, more simply, as "prefiguration," Ricoeur's focus is on the way any individual consciousness inhabits its culture as a symbolic whole. In very basic terms, this means that I am able effortlessly to understand, as I understand my native language, the sign systems of my own society. If I walk out of my house in the morning to see a new Rolls-Royce parked in a neighbor's driveway, I instantly perceive that I am looking primarily at something meant as a sign of wealth or status, and only incidentally at a mechanical device for transporting its owner from point A to point B. (What Ricoeur means by "prenarrative" becomes clear, in turn, when we observe that whatever his Rolls-Royce is meant to "say" about my neighbor will also be said about a character in a novel who owns a Rolls-Royce.) At this level, Ricoeur argues, symbolism confers an initial readability on human action.

At the same time, even to speak about an intent behind my neighbor's action is to move in the direction not simply of Aristotle's *mimēsis praxeōs* but of what has been called the *Verstehen* sociology of cultural theorists such as Clifford Geertz. (Ricoeur approvingly quotes one of Geertz's pronouncements: "Culture is public because meaning is.")[1] Here we encounter that more total conception of cultural symbolism that includes law, custom, tradition, religious beliefs and rituals, and every other system that may be seen to belong to any given culture perceived as a symbolic whole. Considered as an action, the buying of a Rolls-Royce belongs to a particular, local, and undoubtedly transient system of signs. But to understand a ritual action, as Ricoeur once says—the elevation of the host in a Roman Catholic Mass, the serving of the unleavened bread at a Passover Seder—is to understand the meaning of the ritual, which in turn implies an entire system of beliefs, values, and institutions. At this point we are very close to the notion of culture in its entirety as a symbolic system.

In *Time and Narrative*, the conception of culture as symbolic system is important most often as it provides a necessary context for interpreting human action. Even at the Mimesis₁ level of "preunderstanding," where we have a great distance yet to go before getting to Aristotle's *mimēsis praxeōs*, Ricoeur is already deeply concerned with a semantics of action that must be observable, as he sees it, in anything that could be called a human community. For to count as an action, what would otherwise be mere physical movement must be understood within a context involving volition, motives, and goals. My scratching my ear when it itches is not, from this point of view, an action, nor is sneezing, or coughing, or anything I might do while sleepwalking. My going to the refrigerator to get a cold drink on a hot day is an action, but my dog's going to his water dish under what might be seen as exactly similar circumstances is, from the same point of view, something else, an instinctual response to a purely physiological sensation.

This is not to deny that I, as much as my dog, might be experiencing the physical sensation of thirst. But that is not the only reason I might be going to the refrigerator. I might, for instance, be trying to cover over an awkward moment in a conversation I have just been having with you, or making a sociable gesture because friends have just arrived, though I am not in the least thirsty myself. Or, alternatively, I might be thirsty but still going to the refrigerator for one of these other reasons. The idea of a reason for acting, to borrow the title of G. F. Schueler's well-known treatise, covers a very great range of goals, motivations, and circumstances, any of which might be plausibly attributed to a human agent in such a situation. These are precisely what cannot be attributed to the dog as it goes to its water dish. In his *Philosophical Investigations*, Wittgenstein playfully pretends to a wide-eyed naivete as a means of illustrating the same point: "Why can't a dog simulate pain? Is he too honest?"

The idea of a semantics of action matters most importantly to Ricoeur not simply because I might have any number of reasons for going to the refrigerator, but also because those same reasons are necessarily the means we use to explain to ourselves the actions of other people. Here we are in the vicinity of what Aristotle, in the *Poetics*, calls the probable. If the day is hot and I am alone in the house, a neighbor who happens to look through the window will probably conclude that

I have taken a cold drink from the refrigerator because I'm thirsty. One of Aristotle's points, however, is that probability shifts with the circumstances. If you and I are having a conversation painful to us both, and if at a particularly awkward moment I get up to get a drink, you might very well conclude that my action had more to do with an intolerable sense of embarrassment than with thirst.

Even so simple a scenario permits us to see why Ricoeur wants to insist that the ways we understand each other in daily life involve an irreducible narrativity. For your explanation of why I went to the refrigerator is in some elementary sense a story: we were both embarrassed, and to get over the awkwardness he got up and went to get a cold drink. In such moments, Ricoeur thinks, lies the genesis of Aristotle's conception of *mythos* as a mode of explanation by emplotment. Ordinary life, Aristotle said, is most often made up of actions and events that take place in meaningless succession: "one thing after another." But narrative always involves, due to the logic of emplotment, a strong implication of causality: "one thing because of another." The same point is implicit in E. M. Forster's well-known aphorism in *Aspects of the Novel*. "The king died and then the queen died," said Forster, is a chronicle. "The king died and the queen died of grief" is a story.

What is the logic of emplotment that permits a narrative sequence to imply causality? This is a problem to which *Time and Narrative* will devote a great deal of attention in the course of its long and intricate argument, but even at the early stage of Mimesis$_1$, two important principles stand out clearly. The first is that emplotment permits an intuitive grasping together (*prendre ensemble*) of otherwise heterogeneous elements, by which Ricoeur will always mean events occurring in separate orders of reality. To ask how the drink I fetch from the refrigerator came to be cold, for instance, is to invite an explanation in terms of the kinetic behavior of gas molecules under compression. To ask why I am thirsty—if that is the reason I am fetching the drink—is to ask about a physiological sensation in terms of the endocrine response to cellular dehydration. To ask why a sense of embarrassment has led me to get up, on the other hand—an event occurring in a purely psychological realm of social interaction—is implicitly to demand an explanation in terms of human or group psychology.

How, then, does emplotment permit us to grasp occurrences at such heterogeneous levels in a single moment of intuition? The answer takes us to the second of Ricoeur's major principles, which he most often calls "discordant concordance," counting on his readers to recognize his invocation of the *concordia discors* of ancient philosophy. For Heraclitus and Empedocles, thinking in terms of a Greek physics that pictured the material universe as a war of contending elements—earth, air, fire, and water engaged in perpetual struggle—this was an attempt to understand how such elements could coexist harmoniously in such obviously unified entities as flowers, trees, animals, or the human body. Even today, in the age of modern science, something of the same perplexity may occasionally be felt. I am convinced, intellectually, that every atom now in my body circulated billions of years ago in the interior of distant stars, but understanding how they came to form the hand that is writing this sentence—or, even more oddly, how they are related to the sense of intellectual purpose now moving the pen across the page—seems to ask for some different mode of explanation.

Nonetheless, to call a harmonious relation among heterogeneous elements *concordia discors*, as the ancients did, is only to give a name to something that remains to be explained. For Ricoeur, the explanation of emplotment as discordant concordance lies in the concept of *mythos* or plot as a teleological principle: the inexorable movement that drives the story toward an anticipated conclusion. As we shall see, *Time and Narrative* treats this movement as a purely formal consequence of narrative structure, and in particular of what I shall be calling the double temporality of narrative. At the moment, what matters is that both the conclusion and its anticipation count as what might be called objective correlates of the "grasping together" that Ricoeur sees as central to the logic of narrative causality. The *telos* of the plot may be viewed, at this preliminary stage, simply as an ordering principle with a power to suspend or neutralize what might otherwise seem to be troublesome questions about a vast heterogeneity of motives, goals, actions, and material circumstances.

The reason that motives and goals become central to Ricoeur's argument at this point is that he views narrative emplotment as always grounded in what he calls a preunderstanding of the world of action. At the most basic level, as we have seen, this means that your attempt to understand why I have gone to the refrigerator may well take the form of a story about our mutual embarrassment. But it also means that, at the level of social existence, events in ordinary life will strike many of us as stories waiting to be told. And it means, at a further extension, that certain striking episodes will crystalize and pass into collective or communal consciousness, as in the stories of Robin Hood or William Tell or Patrick Henry. This last is no doubt what Roland Barthes had in mind in pointing out, in a celebrated essay on semiotic theory, that "narrative occurs in all periods, all places, all societies; narrative begins with the very history of humanity; there is not, there has never been, any people anywhere without narrative. . . . Narrative is international, transhistorical, transcultural; it is there, like life."[2]

Throughout Aristotle's *Poetics*, as Ricoeur remarks, a sense that works such as *Oedipus Rex* emerge from something very like a collective consciousness is strongly implicit. This is why, for instance, Aristotle is able to praise tragedy for using historical names, like Oedipus and Agememnon, not because they are historical but because they carry in themselves a strong suggestion of probability. What has been, Aristotle says, becomes probable as soon as it is conceived as having actually happened. He is not making a claim about historical veracity. As with certain subjects, such as the Trojan War or the house of Atrides, such names serve as reminders that the story is rooted in a cultural past from which all stories ultimately derive—a common humanity that, much as in Barthes' account of a primordial narrativity, precedes tribe or nation or historical epoch. This, too, is part of what Ricoeur takes Aristotle to mean in saying that *poiēsis*, as opposed to history, which is tied to the singular or particular event, possesses universality.

It is clear from Aristotle's discussion of emplotment that while *Oedipus Rex* counts for him as a preeminent example of *poiēsis*, the Robin Hood ballads would not. The reason is that Sophoclean tragedy possesses what Aristotle calls unity, an abstract structure of beginning, middle, and end that creates a new and self-contained reality in a way that tales and legends sedimented in cultural memory need not. For Ricoeur, this structure—what by linguistic analogy might be called a deep structure of narrative grammar—is actually the abstract object of imitation in Aristotle's *mimēsis praxeōs*, the universal or recurring human event that it is the purpose of *poiēsis* to represent. In life, we remember Aristotle saying, one thing follows another. I get up, I check my mail, I go back for a second cup of coffee. In *poiēsis*, one thing happens because of another. Oedipus puts out his own eyes because the terrible double revelation of parricide and incest has made it intolerable to look any longer on a world in which he has done such things.

Where does the Aristotelian unity that makes *Oedipus Rex* a self-contained whole (*holos*) come from? Aristotle contrasts the arbitrary unity of a single temporal period, in which numerous unrelated things happen to a multitude of people, to the artistic or poetic unity that comes from positing an internal logic of events. In the same way, he praises Homer for having omitted many extraneous elements of the Odysseus legend so as to make the *Odyssey* a single story of epic or heroic return. The *holos* in this sense always implies a logic of development that is not, as Ricoeur says, taken from experience, which is why Aristotle's beginning, middle, and end must be viewed as effects of the ordering of the poem rather than features of some real action. Yet a problem remains. There is obviously a strong conception of narrative causality at work here, but, as most readers of the *Poetics* will recall, Aristotle says little that serves to illuminate it. A beginning, he unhelpfully remarks, is what does not follow something else by causal necessity. An end is what follows something else but has nothing following it. A middle comes between the two.

This is where Ricoeur's analysis crosses the dividing line between Mimesis₁—again, the level of "prefiguration," or the prenarrative structure of ordinary experience—and Mimesis₂, where his subject will be the logic of narrative causality implicit in Aristotle's scheme. For where Aristotle saw an essentially spatial structure, with beginning, middle, and end as parts of a simultaneous whole, Ricoeur sees a structure that is at once spatial and temporal: a chain of causal implication that must be traversed in time, and in a state of partial or imperfect knowledge, before there dawns any intimation that these same events might also be seen as a unity of action. This is the level of what Aristotle calls *peripeteia* or reversal, those changes of fortune during which characters like Oedipus find themselves caught up in developments they try vainly, and often with a growing sense of desperation, to understand. An important point for Ricoeur is that any audience outside the horizon of the events in the story—the original spectators at an Athenian festival, say, or a modern reader of *Oedipus Rex*—must make this traversal in just the same state of imperfect knowledge as those inside it.

Yet Aristotle was not mistaken to see this in terms of spatial structure, for it is that as well. Ricoeur has from the beginning, we recall, described emplotment as a *telos* or movement toward a destined or predetermined end. As one looks back on a completed series of events in a plot, it does seem as though there is something like unity or simultaneity in the causal chain. Within the horizon of the story, the moment that the plot reveals itself as *telos* is what Aristotle called *anagnorisis*, or recognition—in *Oedipus Rex*, that moment of terrible clarity when everyone sees that *this* outcome, though wholly unforeseeable from any previous perspective, was inevitable all along. Then, once again, there is outside the horizon of the story an audience that experiences its own version of this moment of sudden clarity. The logic of narrative causality involves a paradox we encounter in every version of emplotment, from *Oedipus Rex* to the detective stories we read in bed: no, it was entirely unforeseeable; yes, we now see that it was inevitable after all.

The perspective from which Aristotle sees events in *Oedipus Rex* as a simultaneous whole is much more, Ricoeur argues, than a way of looking at narrative structure. For what Aristotle was seeing, whether or not he recognized it as such, was an invariant coordinate of narrative discourse, something built right into the logic of emplotment at the level of *poiēsis*, which here may be taken to include detective stories or other popular fiction as much as Sophoclean tragedy. The perspective Ricoeur wants to isolate resembles, as he notes, the one that Boethius, trying to imagine how God would view the universe, called the *totum simul*: a gaze from outside the limits of human temporality that is able to take in creation, from beginning to end, as a single timeless whole. The difference is that the *totum simul* is not, for Ricoeur, a theological conjecture but, as it operates within narrative structure, a continuous implication of plot during the time that events in the story are unfolding. The originality with which he develops the idea in *Time and Narrative* makes this one of Ricoeur's own important contributions to narratology.

The *totum simul* is, then, essential to Ricoeur's account of the double temporality of narrative structure. Every story, as he later demonstrates in his analysis of both historical and fictional narrative, is in an important sense told forward and backward ("d'avant en arrière et d'arrière en avant") at the same time.[3] The forward movement, which belongs to what Ricoeur calls the syntagmatic order of discourse, links a movement from event X to event Y in an irreducibly temporal way: "The King died, and then the Queen died of grief." This is Aristotle's *mythos* as the logic of emplotment that creates a narrative whole, linking such heterogeneous elements as agent, motive, and circumstance together in a single intelligible order of events. At the same time, any continuous implication that the story has *already* been grasped as a whole—as we shall shortly see, an implication necessarily at work whenever a narrator tells a story in the past tense—means that events must be moving toward a conclusion so far unforeseen by its characters and by us as its audience. The moment at which the forward motion of emplotment comes into abrupt collision with the *totum simul* is Aristotle's *anagnorisis*.

In the *Poetics*, Aristotle distinguishes between drama, as in his analysis of *Oedipus Rex* as *mimēsis praxeōs*, and what he calls diegetic narrative, in which, as in Homer's *Iliad* or *Odyssey*, the story is told by a narrator who exists outside its horizon of events. In drama, where the *totum simul* perspective has been almost entirely absorbed into emplotment, it is normally implied by elements within the dramatic structure, as with the oracle that has foretold a destined outcome, or premonitions experienced by characters in moments of fear or anxiety, or the Chorus that views events and draws its conclusions as the detached observer of the main action. In diegetic narrative, on the other hand, which stretches from Homeric epic in Aristotle's day to works such as Joyce's *Ulysses* or Proust's *À la recherche du temps perdu* in our own, the *totum simul* is always associated with the narrator's perspective on the story he is telling, giving its double temporality a continuous visibility. For this reason, Ricoeur chooses to concentrate mainly on diegetic narrative throughout his own argument.

Ricoeur's analysis of the *totum simul* perspective begins in what narratologists like Harald Weinrich have called the preterite family of narrative tenses, namely, all those verbs—imperfect, perfect, pluperfect, and so on—that in themselves indicate that the action has taken place in a past relative to the time of utterance. In English, this gives us the normal third-person narrative past of the Victorian novel, as at the beginning of Dickens's *A Tale of Two Cities*: "It was the best of times, it was the worst of times." In this case, the times being talked about are the years immediately preceding the French Revolution, gazed upon from the vantage point of a narrator living in mid-nineteenth century England, but the identical structure is also present in the case of first-person narratives, as when an older Nick Carraway looks back on the younger self who was Gatsby's bemused neighbor in *The Great Gatsby*. Within this narrative structure, as Ricoeur says, the events of the story always take place within the past of the narrative voice.

The same structure generates what I have called the double temporality of narrative as Ricoeur conceives it. For within the horizon of events, the story told in *A Tale of Two Cities* or *The Great Gatsby* will move forward in the sequence of ordinary time: *a* happened, then *b*, then *c*. Yet intimations of a *totum simul* in the narrative voice—a structuring of narrative time that highlights certain events so as to imply a chain of narrative causality known to the storyteller but as yet unknown to the listener or reader—will serve as a continuous reminder that the story is already being grasped as a whole. The question of "voice" then becomes simply a question about who is telling the story: in *what* narrative consciousness do these events already constitute an intelligible whole? In the same way, the question of point of view, that reliable standby of the college handbooks, will simply be about the relation of *this* narrative consciousness to the events being recounted.

How does the *totum simul* perspective produce that unity that Aristotle saw in the logic of emplotment? The answer lies, once again, in the past tense of narrative discourse, but now in the possibilities of temporal variation made possible by shifts within the preterite group. Thus, for instance, Weinrich, in his *Tempus: Besprochene und erzählte Welt*, is able to show that the imperfect always signals a receding of the narrative content into a background of continuous or ordinary occurrences. In French, this gives us, for instance, Proust's normal use of the imperfect in *À la recherche*: "J'appuyais tendrement mes joues contre les belles joues de l'oreiller." The perfect, on the other hand, signals a completed past action on which, as it stands out against that background, attention is being concentrated. Ricoeur's example is Caesar's *veni, vidi, vinci.* In English, the same effect can be achieved through tense and temporal markers: "I was sitting, as I normally did in the evening, staring into the fire" versus—Ricoeur calls this a *mise en relief* or putting-into-relief— "That night, a knock came suddenly at the door."

For Ricoeur, an important consequence of double temporality in narrative is that it produces not only the unity that Aristotle recognized in *mythos,* but an inescapable sense of the narrated world as a moral or ethical whole. For the narrator who gazes back on events as a *totum simul* is also someone dwelling within a structure of values and beliefs that necessarily entail ethical judgment. Consider the way all these elements—a structured temporality, emplotment as *telos,* ethical implication—combine when the narrator of Dickens's *A Tale of Two Cities* comes to deal with the outbreak of the French Revolution. It is a sobering moment, as a narrator who has so far invariably shown a deep and anguished sympathy with the plight of dire poverty and exploitation that has led the populace to revolt is compelled to acknowledge an equal sympathy for the innocent victims of indiscriminate social frenzy:

> There was no pause, no pity, no peace, no interval of relenting rest, no measurement of time. Though days and nights circled as regularly as when time was young, and the evening and morning were the first day, other count of time there was none. Hold of it was lost in the raging fever of a nation, as it is in the fever of one patient. Now, breaking the unnatural silence of a whole city, the executioner showed the people the head of the king—and now, it seemed almost in the same breath, the head of his fair wife. . . .
>
> And yet, observing the strange law of contradiction which obtains in all such cases, the time was long, while it flamed by so fast. A revolutionary tribunal in the capital, and forty or fifty thousand revolutionary committees all over the land; . . . prisons gorged with people who had committed no offence, and could obtain no hearing; these things became the established order and nature of appointed things, and seemed to be ancient usage before they were many weeks old.[4]

Finally, in *A Tale of Two Cities*, as in other fictional narratives, the continuous use of the past tense announces that the story is wholly imaginary and that, as such, it constitutes an autonomous or self-contained world. For Weinrich, whose analysis of tense structure in narrative began with the question of what could be said about a past tense that turned out to refer to no actual past, this is a fundamental principle of literary autonomy. In fiction, says Weinrich, the primary function of tenses in the preterite group is precisely to signal a break between the narrated world and any actual or historical time: "The space in which fictional narrative unfolds is not the past."[5] Yet from the "once upon a time" that introduces a fairy tale to invocations of the heavenly Muse in epic, narrative has always had conventions meant as a signal to listeners or readers that they were about to enter an imaginary reality. For Ricoeur, the important point will be that fictional narrative—unlike history, which, as we shall see, is always for him an irreducibly narrative mode as well—has and uses such means to insist in purely formal terms on its own fictionality.

In the *Poetics*, Aristotle speaks of *Oedipus Rex* and other Greek tragedies as works that, just as they had their origins in an earlier body of myth and legend, survive now in the permanence of written form to pass back into communal consciousness as part of an ongoing cultural heritage. The equivalent in the English-speaking world would be, no doubt, Shakespearean drama, as it has provided a common point of reference, or even what might be called a basis of invisible community, among readers through successive generations. Yet for Ricoeur the great point about *Oedipus Rex* or *Paradise Lost* or *Madame Bovary* is not that they are taken back up into the culture within which they originated, but that they are also available in the timelessness of their literary autonomy—Horace's *aere perennius*, Shakespeare's "Not marble, nor gilded monuments"—to a humankind that possesses a universal power to grasp narrative reality. "All classes," says Barthes in the essay already cited, "all human groups, have their narratives, and very often these are enjoyed by men of different, even opposing, culture."[6]

The notion of listeners or readers far distant in time or language or culture from a work's original audience takes us into the region of Ricoeur's Mimesis$_3$, by which he means the total act of comprehension—he calls this "refiguration"—through which a story comes to life in the consciousness of those outside its imaginary world. A crucial point is that this always begins as a matter of purely formal projection, a special instance of the power of language to posit a reality existing independent of discourse. Ricoeur is drawing here on Émile Benveniste's theory of discourse, for which even a simple utterance like "Shut the door!" is intelligible only as it is understood to refer to an immediate and separate physical environment that includes, at a minimum, a room or building or other enclosed space. In narrative, it is the entire set of conventions signaling the immemorial situation in which someone is telling and listening to a story—as in, again, the "once upon a time" of fairy tales or *Märchen*—that projects a world with a potentially limitless set of listeners or readers who may come to join its audience so long as the written work survives the vicissitudes of historical time.

In general terms, Ricoeur's account of Mimesis$_3$ might thus be thought to involve something like Wolfgang Iser's notion of the "implied reader," and, as we shall see in chapter 6, Ricoeur does in fact dutifully mention Iser at several points. Yet "refiguration" demands a far greater respect for the claims of literary autonomy than is evident in Iser's *The Act of Reading*, and Ricoeur takes great pains to ensure that his presentation of Mimesis$_3$ does not dissolve into a mere psychology of reader response. This is an extremely delicate moment in his argument. On the one hand, Mimesis$_3$ demands a conception of audience that is a purely formal projection—a "virtual site" of literary comprehension, as Jonathan Culler once put it.[7] On the other hand, it also demands readers who belong wholly to a world where people eat and drink and, as no purely formal projection can, suffer pain and grow old and die. Ricoeur's point will simply be that, while those whose consciousness is altered by *Oedipus Rex* or *Don Quixote* or *A Tale of Two Cities* may constitute a minority in any given population, that alteration must also take place in a world they know themselves to share with other beings subject to time and mortality.

At a later point in *Time and Narrative*, Ricoeur speaks of every encounter with narrative as a struggle or contest between opposing spheres of reality, a confrontation between what he calls the fictive world of the text and the actual world of the reader. Here, however, in his account of Mimesis$_3$, he wants to emphasize the way in which the semantics of action he earlier discussed at the level of Mimesis$_1$ provides the means of moving back and forth freely between one sphere of reality and the other. As what we have heard Ricoeur call a prenarrative structure of experience, Mimesis$_1$ takes on importance not simply because we inevitably make up stories to explain the motives and actions of others to ourselves, or even because doing so represents an elementary version of the more elaborate logic of emplotment that we encounter in works like *A Tale of Two Cities*. It is important because the characters in whose company we move inside the world of Dickens's story—Charles Darnay and Sydney Carton and Madam Defarge and Jerry Cruncher—think and act in terms wholly familiar to us in ordinary life, which, as Ricoeur's earlier account of Mimesis$_1$ has taught us to see, is rooted in the same semantics of action as the world of the novel.

When we are inside the world of *A Tale of Two Cities*, following the story thus means understanding the narrative causality that sustains its plot, that chain of seemingly inevitable events that commentators, from Aristotle to modern semioticians such as A. J. Greimas, have wanted to see in structural or spatial terms. Against this view, Ricoeur wants to insist that the process of following a story at the level of Mimesis$_3$ is irreducibly temporal, involving that state of partial or imperfect knowledge on the part of both characters and audience that would lose its entire point if the moment of *anagnorisis* as sudden clarification had been known from the outset. Ricoeur's point here has nothing to do with whether one knows how the story will in fact turn out: a Sherlock Holmes story like *The Hound of the Baskervilles* can be read and reread many times with, if anything, increased enjoyment. What is at stake is a cognitive process, the movement from imperfect knowledge to a total clarity that lays bare a new and alternative landscape of reality. Here lies the basis of what Ricoeur means by calling Mimesis$_3$ a "refiguration."

By refiguration Ricoeur means, too, an alteration in consciousness that derives less from a new way of seeing reality than from the impossibility, after reading *King Lear* or *Rasselas* or *Middlemarch*, of *not* seeing it that way. Mimesis$_3$ in this sense bears some resemblance to those alterations in perception conventionally associated with paradigm shifts in the history of science. We can imagine, at any rate, a educated person at the end of the sixteenth century gazing at the night sky and seeing the orderly Ptolemaic universe—crystalline spheres carrying the sun, moon, and planets around a fixed or stationary earth—that his father and grandfather had gazed upon before him. And we can imagine the same person some years later, having learned about Copernicus and Galileo and a new universe in which the earth revolves on its own axis while traveling around the sun, gazing wonderingly on a night sky that is at once the same and radically different. Something like this notion of radical alteration in the context of the same is also implied in Ricoeur's conception of Mimesis$_3$ as refiguration.

The ultimate object of imitation in Aristotle's *mimēsis praxeōs* thus becomes, in Ricoeur's theory of mimesis, that sudden change from imperfect knowledge to *anagnorisis* or recognition that the *Poetics* had identified in merely local terms with a feature of Greek tragic plot. The point of the arc of operations that Ricoeur traces from Mimesis$_1$ to Mimesis$_3$, from a prenarrative structure of experience that exists in every human community to the alteration brought about in individual consciousness by narrative experience, is to suggest that what *poiēsis* imitates is not action itself but a certain abstract structure present in a multiplicity of meaningful actions, and given lasting visibility in a thousand narratives composed in numerous languages and a great variety of cultures. Yet all converge on that alteration of consciousness—what David Parker has called the "epistemic gain" of narrative experience[8]— that Ricoeur sees as the culminating moment in the process of refiguration he calls Mimesis$_3$.

In the *Poetics*, Aristotle famously associates the events leading to *anagnorisis* with a purging of pity and fear in the spectators of tragedy. Ricoeur's more elaborate theory of mimesis suggests an alternative possibility, which is that the clarification brought about by *Madame Bovary* or *Eugene Onegin* or *The Sun Also Rises* may be carried back into the ordinary or everyday world in the altered consciousness of at least some readers. Yet this is not, for Ricoeur, an inevitable consequence of narrative experience. Other readers might, after all, remain unmoved by any given story. Another consequence, to which *Time and Narrative* will devote a great deal of attention, is both inevitable and universal. It is that readers who have dwelt for a certain interval in the imaginary world inhabited by Emma or Tatiana or Lady Brett, a reality that will also exist and be available to other readers a century or more from now, then inevitably return to a world where everything that lives must grow old and die. This is the point at which Ricoeur takes up the central philosophical problem addressed by his argument, which is on exactly what terms the seemingly timeless world of narrative can be understood to exist in a world of mortal time.

Chapter Two

TIME

AT THE BEGINNING OF *TIME AND NARRATIVE*, RICOEUR SUMMARIZES a well-known skeptical paradox about time, which is that past, present, and future, its three primary constituents, dissolve under scrutiny into nothingness. The past, by universal agreement, is what no longer exists. The future is not yet. And the present, which can seem to have some substance even as a continuously vanishing "now," turns out on closer inspection to be purely relational, something like the "line" that separates a black silhouette on white paper from its background, but cannot be shown to be some third thing that is neither black nor white. In discussing the illusion of the "now," Ricoeur makes a point of recalling Augustine's discovery that "the present cannot possibly have duration." For it was the skeptical argument, leading to the ontological question *quid enim est tempus*, that prompted Augustine's famous cry of perplexity in his *Confessions*: "What, then, is time? I know well enough what it is, provided that nobody asks me; but if I am asked what it is and try to explain, I am baffled."[1]

Still, Ricoeur is only tangentially concerned with the skeptical paradox. His concern in *Time and Narrative* is with the problem of intelligible order in the universe, which the paradox of time happens to present in a particularly arresting way. At the root of the problem lies the possibility that human consciousness dwells in lonely isolation in a blind material universe, a mere whirl of objects in senseless motion, that is wholly oblivious to its existence. The notion of intelligibility

19

arises as the possibility that there might be an underlying order—the *logos* of the ancient Stoics, say, or the mathematical equations on view in Newton's *Principia* or Einstein's theory of relativity—that makes the universe something more than a senseless whirl of substance. With this, however, comes the question of whether the laws governing matter are "in" the universe: meteorites and cosmic dust, one wants to say, would surely go on obeying Newton's inverse-square law of gravitation even if all human consciousness were suddenly annihilated. Yet this, too, has an air of paradox about it. Mathematics and scientific laws can seem, after all, to have some irreducible relation to consciousness. We do seem to have a persistent intuition that no meteorite could possibly know about the laws governing its own motion in space.

As his spokesman for the position that time is inherent in the physical universe, Ricoeur takes the Aristotle of the *Physics*, who associates temporality with the movement of the sun, moon, planets, and stars through the sky. One sees readily enough why Aristotle imagined that time must have an independent existence: if humans were subtracted from the world, the heavenly bodies would continue to travel their celestial round. Ricoeur calls this cosmic or cosmological time, and, in the latter stages of his argument, the "time of the world." His spokesman for the opposing view that time is constituted by human consciousness—the view that if consciousness were subtracted from the universe, time would vanish along with it, leaving only the blind processes associated with motion—is Augustine. Ricoeur will normally call this phenomenological time, but sometimes, and again mainly in the latter stages of his argument, the "time of the soul." Ricoeur's own position will be that both views, along with versions to be found in such later philosophers as Kant and Husserl, lead to irresolvable paradox.

The paradox occurs because, as Ricoeur demonstrates in patient detail, any attempt to prove that cosmic time could exist independent of consciousness will proceed by smuggling in some element of phenomenological perception. Aristotle does this, for instance, by silently assuming that certain irreducibly phenomenological elements—time, for instance, as measured by a "before," "after," and "now"—would persist even if human consciousness were missing from the universe. For Augustine, on the other hand, the paradox takes the form of smuggling in elements of the physical universe while trying to show that temporality may be wholly generated by consciousness. (Husserl, as we shall see, does a version of the same thing at a somewhat higher level of philosophical sophistication.) This move of Augustine's is, Ricoeur argues, inevitable, since the notion of time existing for a consciousness wholly cut off from a world external to itself is incoherent. One sees the point. Someone confined to an white windowless room and kept from all contact with the outside would, it is at least possible to suppose, soon enough be without any meaningful sense of external time.

Aristotle's conception of time as something measured by the movement of heavenly bodies suggests why he saw it as having an independent existence, for it seems evident that what is measured must exist. His analysis in the *Physics* depends on the related notions of movement and magnitude. Movement is primary, as when I see a car appear at the end of my street, move past me, and vanish from sight at the other end. Movement implies magnitude: the space traversed by the car may be measured in yards, feet, and inches. Time will then seem to derive directly from movement when we transfer to it this notion of measurability while adding directionality—a purely spatial concept—and a "before" and "after" that can themselves seem spatial: before the car turned the corner it was invisible to me, as it was after it turned again at the other end. Since we can measure the velocity of the car and the length of the street, the "time" of its passage seems obviously calculable from movement and magnitude alone.

Just as important, it is clearly incidental that the car is being driven by anyone: a robot vehicle directed by programmed instructions from a satellite could make just the same traversal of the street. It is true that I am present as a human observer, but that seems equally incidental. All would have happened in exactly the same way if a robot-driven vehicle had passed down the street unobserved. Even so, it is evident that a phenomenological element persists in Aristotle's analysis, for as soon as we ask *who* is to do the measuring, a notion of mind or consciousness seems unavoidably to enter the picture again. Aristotle, as Ricoeur points out, was uneasily aware of the problem, even going so far to ask at one point if "time would exist if the soul did not exist." Still, he wants to maintain that consciousness in such cases is simply "taking up" a time already present in external reality, just as the width and breadth of a table must really be there before I could measure them with a yardstick.

Why was Aristotle determined, in the last analysis, to see time as something wholly independent of consciousness? The answer, Ricoeur thinks, is that the Greek notion of *physis* (nature) strongly implied a *subjection* of consciousness to nature. No conception of time as produced or generated from within human consciousness could, given this view, account for a sense of time as a power governing processes of growth and decay that lie outside human control. This is time in that half-mythic aspect that Ricoeur will refer to as Time the Destroyer, a conception that haunts philosophy and literature—"at my back I always hear Time's wingèd chariot hurrying near"—from the beginnings of both. Aristotle notes, but does nothing to elucidate, the problem when he observes that "all things grow old in time." Thus, time on his conception appears as a form of change that for unexplained reasons moves inexorably toward deterioration and decay.

In modern philosophy, the counterpart of Aristotle's cosmological time is to be found, Ricoeur argues, in Kant. On the face of it this is surprising, since it was precisely Kant's account of time as an inner intuition—that is, an empty grid imposed by the mind on the raw flux of experience—that underlay what Kant called his Copernican revolution in philosophy: "If we take away from our inner intuition the peculiar condition of our sensibility, the concept of time likewise vanishes; it does not inhere in the objects, but merely in the subject which intuits them."[2] This in turn explains the central rule of Kant's method, which is that such things as space and time—and even, as in the doctrine of *Selbstaffektion*, mind or consciousness itself—must never be sought as direct objects of experience, but can only be brought to light, through painstaking analysis, as conditions of possibility for what appears to us as the world external to our perception.

Kant's analysis of space as what he calls an outer intuition is a particularly elegant example of the method. By "sensibility" in the sentence quoted above Kant means "our ability to be affected by objects": that is, our having indubitable ground for assuming, at a minimum, some real relation to a world of tables and chairs and trees and stars. But our sense that space belongs to this world is an illusion: take away the empty form of outer intuition and, Kant says, "the representation of space stands for nothing whatsoever." Kant's demonstration in *The Critique of Pure Reason* that space is "nonempirical" may be seen through a thought experiment in which the empirical contents of outward perception are gradually subtracted. So, for instance, I look up at the night sky and see not only planets and stars and galaxies but the space that stretches between or among them. And I can imagine those objects vanishing one by one until only the space is left. It is when I ask myself what would then exist if that space vanished—more space? a different space? a "nothing" that was not itself space?—that I grasp what Kant means by calling space an a priori intuition.

Ricoeur's point will be that this same procedure fails when Kant tries to use a version of it in relation to time. Kant begins with the appearance of any two events—a knock comes at the door, let us say, while a plane passes overhead—about which we can say that they were simultaneous or successive. So far, we are on solid a priori ground: events must, we can confidently say even before they happen, occur either at the same time or one after another. But then we must also be able to say that their occurrence took place in relation to some third thing that gives meaning to the notions of simultaneity and succession. They must, says Kant, be given "an underlying ground which exists *at all times*, that is, something *abiding* and *permanent*."[3] Like space when we emptied the sky of its contents, time is what remains. The problem, as Ricoeur points out, is that this notion of empty or "timeless" time leaves no way of accounting for temporal order or duration.

Kant tried to solve the problem by relating time to causality, which for him was another of the contentless forms imposed by the mind on the world of objects. Ricoeur provides a detailed demonstration of why the attempt fails, but its point is that Kant finally succeeds only in reformulating Aristotle's cosmic time in terms of a new Enlightenment empiricism, based on a Newtonian universe of time, space, and causality existing independent of lived or mortal time. Kant's argument then runs aground on the problem of duration, Ricoeur argues, precisely because, in a Newtonian universe, time can only exist as mere successive "instants" that are indistinguishable from one another in terms of anything internal to their succession. We could imagine, by way of illustration, an eternally swinging pendulum moving through a perpetual arc. It is clear that we have succession here—one movement does follow another—but not yet clear that we have either time or duration, both of which spring into existence only when we impose a "now" of lived experience on one of its interchangeable instants and proceed to keep count within the separate sphere of our consciousness.

The repressed element of phenomenological perception in Aristotle and Kant takes us back to Augustine, to whom the dependence of time on human consciousness seemed self-evidently a more convincing alternative. Augustine was wholly aware of the argument for cosmological time—though, as Ricoeur points out, in an oversimplified form that leaves out Aristotle's careful qualifications. He had once heard a learned man say, Augustine tells us in book 11 of the *Confessions*, that time was nothing but the movement of the sun and the moon and the stars. But he did not agree. The reason for his disagreement involves an exemplary bit of logical analysis. The sun and the moon and the stars are, by universal agreement, bodies in motion. We can, in turn, imagine anything that is a body in motion speeding up or slowing down. So: if time is identical with the movement of the heavenly bodies, and if the heavenly bodies were to speed up or slow down, what could then account for our ability to say that any one of them had taken "more time" or "less time" to complete its circuit than previously?

How, then, can we account for our ability to measure time, or counter the standard argument that anything that can be measured must exist? Augustine's answer may be taken as an early instance of phenomenological method. It is not, he says, external events that we measure, but the impression (*vestigium*) they leave on the mind: "it is the impression that I measure." His great example is the hymn *Deus creator omnium*, which he knows by heart and of which he can measure the length or duration simply by paying attention to what is going on as he recites it. In this case, there are two measures of duration, the first being the long and short syllables of classical prosody, which give a poetic composition something very like a determinate extension in time. The second, which has to do with the act of consciousness involved in recitation, lies in Augustine's sense, as he proceeds through the poem, that he is getting farther and farther away from its beginning and closer to its end. This is for him the original or primordial form of temporal awareness.

To this primordial structure of perception Augustine gives the name *distentio animi*, a "stretching out" of mind or consciousness in the opposite directions that, in the mode of a fully constituted temporality, will be called past and future. An important point of Augustine's argument, however, is that this stretching-out is not so far temporal. As I write this sentence, for instance, I am continuously aware—though when writing I don't normally pay attention to this sort of thing—that I am moving steadily farther and farther away from its first word, and also that, until I reach the period that signals its completion, there is more to come. Out of this "moving away from" and "more to come," Augustine argues, is born the notion of independently existing time, which materializes when I have learned to say in conventional terms that the earlier parts of my sentence are "receding into the past" and the part not yet written still "lies in the future."

The modern counterpart of Augustine's argument is Husserl's analysis of time-consciousness, which he initiates with the standard phenomenological move of suspending or bracketing all questions about an external world, while paying careful attention to an object that exists in or for consciousness. In this case, what Husserl brackets is precisely Aristotle's "world time": the time of physics or cosmology. In its place, he examines time as it reveals itself to be internal to the flow of consciousness itself, which on his view then makes possible the subsequent constitution of "objective" time. His analysis begins on grounds that are very nearly Kantian. There are certain a priori features evident, he points out, from any preliminary consideration of time-consciousness, for instance, that two different times must be nonsimultaneous—or they would be "the same" time—or that every time carries with it an "earlier" and "later." So much belongs simply to what might be called the logical grammar of time.

Husserl's aim is to provide an account of duration, which Ricoeur sees as presenting the main obstacle to Kant's concept of time as an inner intuition. As what he calls his *Zeitobjekt*, or "time object," Husserl takes a sound: a single musical note, as it might be, that begins, continues, and ceases. The example is brilliantly chosen, for a sound as *Zeitobjekt* is simply sensed rather than perceived. If I am looking at an object or objects in space—a cube, a building, a landscape—all sorts of considerations about the external world enter into an investigation of my perception, as with what Husserl calls "empty intentions": for example, my conviction, as I look at the building from one side, that there are more sides, which I would see if I walked all the way around it. But I simply *hear* the sound. It might even be, as in the case of a medical condition like tinnitus, a "sound" produced by neurological processes in my brain and corresponding to nothing in the physical environment. The only crucial fact for Husserl's purposes is that it is independent of me: my will has no power to start or stop it.

As what Husserl calls a pure object of consciousness, the sound also involves what he calls *retention*. As the term implies, this simply means that so long as it goes on, I can say that the sound is still being heard. But what "still" means in this context turns out to be quite complicated: (1) it "is itself" (I hear "the same sound" from start to finish), but (2) it is also "not itself" (even as I listen, the sound is being swallowed up by a past that no longer exists for my "now"). The word "still" here refers, Husserl points out, as much to my awareness as to the sound itself: the continuous falling off or running away (Husserl's term is *ablaufen*) of the sound in relation to the "now" of my listening consciousness. Husserl's discovery is thus that identity-in-change belongs to consciousness, not in the schematic Kantian sense of being a form imposed on the world, but in the sense that the sound appears as an "object in the mode of running off."

Ricoeur calls Husserl's discovery a "longitudinal intentionality" that preserves the character of the object-as-other. Its principal importance is that it permits Husserl to describe duration as a "retention of retentions." Consider: there is silence, and then I hear a sound. As I listen, I am aware that the sound is passing away, but *also* that there are two notions of "past" involved in my experience: (1) the past that began when the silence was broken (past A, let us call it), and (2) the past that the continuous sound builds up within its own duration as it goes on (past B). Our sense that A is different *in kind* from B is the basis of Husserl's account of duration, retention, and identity-in-change. For my sense that this is "the same" sound derives not simply from a retained awareness of the sound but from a retained awareness of my own sense of it as "the same." The power of consciousness to actually create time thus lies in what Husserl calls a double intentionality, the second intentionality being, so to speak, consciousness perceiving itself in the process of constituting the temporal object.

Nonetheless, Husserl's argument, for all its originality, is in Ricoeur's opinion unsuccessful. Its failure, he argues, is that of every purely speculative attempt to resolve the paradox of time, which is that it will be compelled to introduce, whether from the standpoint of phenomenological or of cosmological time, some unrecognized element of that other temporality it is trying to expose as an illusion. Thus, for instance, Augustine will use the long and short syllables of classical prosody to measure what he thinks is a time of consciousness while forgetting that it is the duration of sounds—bursts of noise as physical events—that makes them long or short. Husserl will take a sound as his *Zeitobjekt* while stipulating that it begins and ceases independent of the will, forgetting that such independence is a minimal description of any object external to consciousness. In the same way, Aristotle, for whom time is the motion of the stars, and Kant, for whom it is the "timeless" ground of inner intuition, will silently and continously appeal to a "now" of lived experience that has, in logical terms, no place in their arguments.

The other major philosopher to whose views *Time and Narrative* devotes a great deal of attention—more, actually, than to any of the others so far discussed—is Heidegger, whose great work *Being and Time* looms over Ricoeur's argument, as it does over so much twentieth-century French philosophy. Yet it is not Heidegger's contribution to the speculative debate about temporality that concerns Ricoeur. Indeed, he considers that contribution to be virtually negligible. For Ricoeur, Heidegger's most important philosophical contribution was his demonstration of the rootedness of temporality in *Sorge*, or care, which in *Being and Time* is said to derive from the sense of finitude or limitation that gives meaning to even the most ordinary human activities. Heidegger's analysis of *Sorge* shifts the ground of debate toward an issue that Ricoeur regards as immensely more important than mere logical paradoxes about time, namely, why and how "meaning" comes to originate in human consciousness.

Heidegger is famous for having invented a new and sometimes unwieldy philosophical vocabulary to get across the perspective of what he called his hermeneutics of Being. Only a few terms are needed to follow the points of Ricoeur's critique of *Being and Time*. The first is *Dasein*, Heidegger's term for the human being. The German word *Dasein* translates simply as "being there": a strange name, it has been remarked, for what we usually call the "I" of human consciousness. But Heidegger means its strangeness to signal an important break with the way we usually think about such things as consciousness and personal identity, and in particular about the "I" as an isolated center of consciousness essentially unconnected to the world. In Heidegger's philosophy, Dasein is essentially *in* the world before it is an "I"—what he would have identified as something like a disembodied Cartesian ego, which comes at a much later stage of abstraction.

In particular, Heidegger means the concept of Dasein to challenge in a radical way any unexamined notion that human beings are simply one more entity among others—rocks, trees, animals, tables, chairs—in the world. His way of putting this is well known: entities have being, but only Dasein has Being, meaning that only for Dasein is its being itself an issue. On the most elementary level, this simply means that I can ask how and why I exist, as a rock or a tree cannot. Yet on a more comprehensive level the notion of "being an issue" extends to everything about which I have the power to choose—in ordinary life, whether I should go to the grocery store now or later, when I have finished my writing for the day, or, in extraordinary circumstances, whether I should stand up for a principle of justice even if it means losing my job or putting myself in physical danger. In the latter case, we are close to what Heidegger speaks of as resoluteness and authenticity.

The context in which even ordinary choices take on meaning or significance for me is, in turn, my "thrownness," by which Heidegger means that I was born into a world at a time and under circumstances over which I had no control. At an elementary level, once again, my being "thrown" into the world involves matters as basic as my physical characteristics—whether I am short-sighted, for instance, or below rather than above average height, or am tone deaf rather than having perfect musical pitch—along with my nationality, my native language, the socioeconomic status of my family, the customs and taboos of my culture, and the like. In a more extended sense, the same thrownness survives throughout my life as a set of circumstances over which I have no control, as when my tone-deafness makes it impossible that I will ever earn a seat in a symphony orchestra.

Dasein not only is born into a world it did not make, but is inevitably brought to an awareness of its finitude. The world into which I was thrown at birth is also one out of which I must someday die. My existence as Dasein is the "betweenness"—the German word is *Erstreckung*, implying a "stretching out"—that separates the two events. In the attitude of Dasein toward its finiteness lies the point of Heidegger's concern with resoluteness and authenticity, which taken together represent the choice not to live on the level of the thoughtless majority who are fleeing their own death by taking refuge in the trivial, the ordinary, or the everyday. In this sense, Heidegger's invocation of such concepts as *Gerede*—the mindless or inconsequential chatter that passes among many people for conversation—is something like an existential counterpart of Pascal's *divertissement*, being, as one might say, a way of getting through life without having lived. The alternative is authenticity, or choosing one's way of being in the world in full consciousness of its finitude.

Heidegger calls the awareness that we are born to die, whether or not it is resolutely confronted, "being toward death." This is the condition that generates *Sorge* or care as a core element of human consciousness. At the level of Heideggerian resolution and authenticity, *Sorge* retains many of the somber connotations of anxiety, sorrow, or fear that the word normally carries in German. At the level of everyday activity, however, the simple sense of *Erstreckung* or "betweenness" is enough to generate *Sorge* as the sense of restricted circumstance that gives the ego an investment in its projects. For *Erstreckung* operates at this level as a structure of limitation imposed on even our most ordinary choices. If I decide, later this morning, to work on the bookshelves I am currently making in my shop, I will be conscious of having chosen to do so against a background of other, excluded choices. For Heidegger—and for Ricoeur, who will call my hour in the workshop a "time of preoccupation"—it is the way *Sorge* determines its engagements with the world that discloses an essential truth about Dasein.

Dasein's investment in its projects gives us the basis of Heidegger's well-known distinction between a reality that is merely *vorhanden* or "present at hand," the neutral or passive background against which any meaningful activity takes place, and one made up of objects that are *zuhanden* or "ready to hand": that is, so absorbed into a structure of present concern that they seem to constitute a separate and more immediate reality. As I am now writing, for instance, I am barely aware—if it weren't for the point I am now making, would probably be completely unaware—of my surroundings: rugs, pictures, lamps, the Civil War musket that hangs on the opposite wall, are all just passive or inertly *vorhanden* in Heidegger's sense of the term. But my pen, the paper on which I write, the volume of *Temps et récit* open before me, are *zuhanden*, so integral to my present concern that they—and I—seem to belong to a single ongoing activity.

The same context of investment in a project gives us the structure from which Heidegger will derive his account of temporality, the "time" of *Being and Time.* As the source of its own projects, Dasein is always "ahead of itself," or oriented toward states of affairs at least partly brought about by its own actions. In the same way, Dasein's actions always involve a "coming toward oneself." This is a structure discernible even at the level of our most trivial activities. When I get up to get a cold drink from the refrigerator, I am "ahead of myself" in the purely formal sense that my action is intelligible in terms of its imagined result. I walk toward the refrigerator, already seeing myself opening the door and taking an iced tea from the shelf at the back. By the same token, having already imagined the drink I am going to fetch, I so to speak meet myself coming the other way as I move toward the refrigerator, which is what Heidegger means by the "coming toward oneself" aspect of my action.

Consider, in light of this analysis, any normal or typical human activity, as when I sow seeds to raise a crop to feed my family. If I were a city dweller taking a rural walk, the surrounding landscape of trees and fields would, in Heidegger's terms, simply exist "alongside" me, as the inert or neutral setting of my inward preoccupation with other matters. It is my investment in my project that transforms it into a landscape of care or concern. The implements I use to prepare the ground are obviously *zuhanden* in Heidegger's sense. In my scattering the seed while thinking about the harvest to come, the features of Dasein's "being ahead of itself" and "coming toward oneself" are both in evidence. In this setting, Heidegger's focus is on the element of *Sorge*—now, perhaps, best translated as "preoccupation," as in the verb *besorgen*—that connects me to the things of a world that no longer sits passively alongside me. That preoccupation here becomes what Heidegger calls a "making present" (*gewärtigen*) that occurs as the result of active involvement in a project.

This is the point at which Ricoeur departs radically from Heidegger on the question of time. He continues to accept Heidegger's analysis of Dasein as original and important—indeed, Ricoeur's own conception of narrative as taking place in a "third time" that is neither that of the world or the soul will owe a great deal to Heidegger—but he also takes as arbitrary and unfounded Heidegger's characterization of external or objective time as involving a fall into inauthenticity. For in *gewärtigen*, that "making present" that occurs whenever I am moving toward or bringing about an already imagined state of affairs, Heidegger saw the beginnings of a false temporality, an objectified and autonomous time that swallows up the *Sorge* from which it derives and blinds Dasein to possibilities of fulfilling itself in the realm of choice and action. According to Heidegger, the objective time of science and of a dehumanized world is produced only through a series of what he calls forgettings.

To understand why Ricoeur rejects this view, it is necessary to follow Heidegger through the steps leading to false temporality. The movement originates, Heidegger thinks, in datability. Dasein does not *begin* by dating things. We may at least suppose that the first humans to sow seed to raise a crop were still very far away from a system of clocks and calendars. Yet when preoccupation gives an apparent substantiality to a "now" that would otherwise have remained a "making present" in a purely relational structure of concern, there suddenly leaps into existence a "no longer" (the ground is "no longer" unplowed) and a "not yet" (the first shoots have "not yet" appeared). The effect is to transfer the entire structure of my investment or concern onto the object-world with which I am engaged, giving rise to a conception of measurable time and calendrical units: "The harvest will be in three months." This is the point at which Aristotle's heavenly bodies begin to assume the aspect of a celestial clock or calendar.

Even at this stage, however, we are still at some distance from an autonomous time of clocks and calendars. The moment at which it occurs to me to measure my seasons of sowing and reaping by the position of the constellations—what might be called the georgic time of Hesiod or Virgil, in which agriculture is still partly understood in religious terms—belongs to the time of *Sorge*. To see how an objectified time gradually disengages itself from the world of human concern or preoccupation, it is necessary to recall that Heidegger's conception of "thrownness," which gives birth to the projects of Dasein, also implies an essential passivity in relation to the object-world. I can plant and hoe and weed, but the harvest will ultimately depend on the sun and rain and other forces outside my control. So, as generations come and go and these external conditions determine either the scantiness or bounty of harvests, the world absorbs the structure of *Sorge* and increasingly gives it back as public time, as a uniform system of intermeasurable "instants" whose origins in care have been forgotten.

From public time, the way is open to the totally objectified time of science and, as Ricoeur says, to a complete divorce from the fundamental structure of Being-in-the-world constitutive of care. The ultimate stage of this concealment is that through which, in identifying time with the objects and processes that surround us, we begin actually to live a relation to time as an autonomous entity. This is what Heidegger will call "ordinary time," whose power to degrade or debase human authenticity he identifies with a process he calls "leveling off." What this means is that the inner topography of the world of care, with its heights and depths—my times of anxious expectation, of pure tedium, of joy or pleasure—are ordered by an external system of interchangeable "nows" that I and everyone else accept as the true measure of temporality. My endless wait to hear whether my loved one survived a crash, as opposed to your two-hours-that-pass-in-a-flash while you are absorbed in a game of chess, are "leveled off" into identical units of an autonomous clock time.

At the level of individual consciousness, leveling off then becomes what might be called a machine for producing inauthenticity. As the origins of time in care are lost, dates are no longer intervals that arose from my preoccupation, for I have learned instead to schedule my preoccupation by dates: "Plant seeds on 26 March." At a further stage of technological development and material production, there emerges the possibility of a robot-like world whose citizens schedule everything by the calendar and the clock, as well as permitting instantaneous communication among multitudes circulating like automata within an identical system of objectified public time. Public time itself, instead of being an aspect of my being-with-others—what Heidegger calls *Mitsein*, in which he sees, under better circumstances, the possibility of an authentic notion of shared or collective destiny—becomes "universal" and apart from me and them. This is the level of what Heidegger calls *Innerzeitigkeit* or "within-timeness," the falsest level of human consciousness.

The missing element in Heidegger's account of temporality, Ricoeur thinks, comes from his failure to deal at any level with the problem of a gap or break between mind or consciousness and the material universe that thinkers as diverse as Augustine and Aristotle and Kant and Husserl had seen as being inseparable from the problem of time. Rather than facing the seeming paradox of a blind universe that somehow possesses time while remaining oblivious to human existence, or the opposing paradox of a human consciousness that somehow understands time without reference to a world external to itself, Heidegger is content, Ricoeur observes, to smuggle in elements of objective time at the earliest stage of his analysis and then unveil them as a series of "forgettings" in the movement toward *Innerzeitigkeit*. Thus, Dasein's "being ahead of itself," for instance, can already be seen to harbor certain features of datability—it seems unlikely that after several seasons of planting my crops, after all, I should fail to notice *some* recurrent markers of seasonal change corresponding to my actions—and with them the beginnings of an inevitable fall into Heidegger's external or "ordinary" time."

What permits Heidegger to avoid the gap between the time of the world and the time of the soul? For Ricoeur, the answer lies in the original move that allowed Heidegger to derive *Sorge* from being-toward-death—that sense of finitude or limitation that gives momentous weight to my choices or, alternatively, to that inauthenticity where I flee my death by living a trivial existence in which I never really think for myself. The notion of being-toward-death in this context is so striking, Ricoeur thinks, that it allowed Heidegger to move unobserved from the time of concern to the time of clocks and calendars, and from there to the inauthentic existence of those souls who dwell perpetually in a state of *Innerzeitigkeit*. At the historical moment in which *Being and Time* appeared—half a century after Nietzsche had announced the death of God, and in the immediate aftermath of that "feast of death," as Thomas Mann called it, that was the Great War—the idea no doubt carried a good deal of intuitive appeal. Yet Ricoeur takes this to be an arbitrary and unfounded element in Heidegger's system.

The fatal weakness of being-toward-death is that, for Heidegger's argument to work, it must be considered a universal element in human experience. Much of the power of *Being and Time* as a philosophical work, and of Heidegger's demonstration of the inevitable situatedness of Being as he describes it, comes from the fact that so many of the features attributed to Dasein do seem to have universal status. We should find it difficult to imagine anything we should want to call a human community whose members did not experience investment in their projects, and were therefore "ahead of themselves" in Heidegger's sense, or who did not experience certain things—whether a stone axe or a modern radial saw—as *zuhanden*, while their surroundings in a time of preoccupation remained merely *vorhanden* or unremarked. Yet one's attitude toward death seems to sit uneasily among these universal attributes, if only because the ways of conceiving of the limitation imposed on Dasein by mortality seem so obviously various, and so clearly relative to the beliefs of one's own tribe or culture or religion.

The key to Ricoeur's rejection of Heidegger's claims for being-toward-death thus lies in that "resoluteness" that *Being and Time* posits as the basis of authenticity. Where Heidegger saw a universal element in human consciousness, Ricoeur sees only a modern neostoicism having affinities with the late Stoicism of such writers as Epictetus or Marcus Aurelius. Within a belief system in which the death of the body is taken to involve a simultaneous annihilation of consciousness—where mind or body is "swallowed up and lost," as Milton's Belial puts it, "in the wide womb of uncreated night"—Heidegger's "resoluteness" makes perfect sense. But it would not have made a great deal of sense, as Ricoeur points out, to Augustine or Pascal or Kierkegaard, for whom it was precisely the conviction that the soul does *not* perish with the body that counted as the basis for choice and action in mortal life. This is why Ricoeur, having arrived at the end of a careful reexamination of Heidegger's account of temporality, proposes setting aside being-toward-death and seeing what else of value remains.

What remains is *Sorge*, or care, in which Ricoeur thinks Heidegger was right to see the ground of meaning as it exists for human consciousness. But its real source lies not in being-toward-death but in that sense of exile in a blind universe that earlier philosophers associated with the paradox of time. In his *Nature*, Ralph Waldo Emerson speaks of "the total disparity between the evidence of our being, and the evidence of the world's being."[4] In *Time and Narrative*, that disparity comes into view whenever we realize that "objective" time is the time of a universe that does not know we exist. This is when the paradox of time—that irresolvable gap between a time of the world and a time of the soul—becomes the gap between an instinctive sense that the world is meaningful and an ineradicable anxiety that it is not. In all human communities, Ricoeur will argue, the way that gap is closed is through a "third time" of narrative, in which consciousness discovers the alternative possibility of an external reality that belongs to the mind or soul alone.

Chapter Three

NARRATIVITY

NARRATIVE, WE RECALL ROLAND BARTHES SAYING, "BEGINS WITH the very history of humanity; there is not, there never has been, any people anywhere without narrative. All classes, all human groups, have their narratives."[1] The philosophical seriousness with which Ricoeur approaches the topic is owing to a similar sense of narrativity—a capacity to understand, tell, and live by and through stories—as a human universal. In *Time and Narrative*, it is not only the ability of people and societies to tell stories, but the power of stories to shape people and societies, that will become his ultimate focus. Like symbol and metaphor, like language itself, narrative is for him inseparable from a conception of anything we should want to mean by a human community. "People have always told stories," he said when asked about *Time and Narrative* in a late interview. "We have here a widespread use of language, so popular and at the same time disclosing such deep connections to life, to other people, and to society as a whole that narrative is an inexhaustible treasure."[2]

At the same time, there are important differences in the way Ricoeur and Barthes think about narrativity. Ricoeur's concept of universality is not unlike Noam Chomsky's notion of innate linguistic competence, which does seem, if only on empirical grounds, to be universal. A child born in Japan, we know, will learn Japanese. The same child, removed at an early age to France or England, will grow up speaking French or English. *Time and Narrative* assumes a similar principle of narrative

competence among people living in any human society. Barthes' remarks on the universality of narrative, on the other hand, were made
in the early period of semiotic or structuralist theory, putting him in
the company of writers such as Claude Lévi-Strauss in anthropology
and Lacan in psychoanalysis, all involved in the larger project that Foucault described as the decentering of the subject. By this he meant the
displacement of human consciousness in relation to various abstract
systems—"the laws of its desire," as Foucault once says, "the forms of
its language, the rules of its actions"[3]—thought to have created or constituted it.

In general terms, Ricoeur's theory of narrative may be taken as an
extended rejoinder to the structuralist ambition that dominated French
intellectual life for several decades in the postwar period. But rejoinder
does not mean outright rejection. To the contrary, one still gets a lively
sense, in the pages of *Time and Narrative*, of the excitement that greeted
Lévi-Strauss's *Elementary Structures of Kinship* in the late 1940s, or the
sense of dawning revelation that Barthes tells us he felt when reading
Ferdinand de Saussure's *Course in General Linguistics* in the mid-1950s.[4]
For much of what semiotics discovered in decentering the subject was
and is, in Ricoeur's opinion, true and important. For him, its limitations
lie in a certain sterility or empty formalism arising from the further
claim that consciousness itself is a mere epiphenomenon of underlying systems. But this does not prevent one from following the logic of
structuralist analysis to its end, absorbing its genuine insights, and rein-
tegrating those insights into a more comprehensive account of volition,
motive, and action.

In standard accounts of structuralism, Saussure's discovery of
meaning as a "negative" effect of differences within a closed system normally counts as the revolutionary element. In the body of narratological work that Ricoeur considers in *Time and Narrative*, however—and
especially, as we shall see, in the work of A. J. Greimas—what matters
most is the way Saussure conceived of language as a rule-governed system, permitting a great variety of linguistic expression to be explained
in terms of a simpler set of underlying constraints. The key notion is
simplicity. The idea that language obeys a determinate set of rules was,
after all, already familiar to the ancient grammarians. But this is not

what Barthes has in mind when he says that "it seems reasonable to take linguistics as a founding model for the structural analysis of narrative."[5] What he means to declare is the possibility of what might be called a grammar of narrative, and the grammar he is thinking of is based on the new Saussurean model he had discovered in the *Cours de linguistique générale.*

To understand what might be meant by a grammar of narrative, it is useful to imagine how an observer who had never heard of the game of chess might go about making sense of a chess tournament. Saussure himself uses the chess analogy for various purposes in the *Cours,* and even speaks at one point about a grammar of chess. From a structuralist viewpoint, it is easy to see why. Given a pencil and notebook and time to watch a large enough sample of games, an attentive observer might be counted upon to remark a set of invariant elements—*this* object always moves on the diagonal, *these* objects either one or two squares initially, and thereafter one square only, and so on—that would lead eventually to the isolation of a relatively simple system of rules governing an otherwise bewildering variety of actual games. Other features of the Saussurean model are on display here—in particular, what Saussure called synchronic as opposed to diachronic analysis—but the magic lies, obviously, in its power to gaze through the enormous complexity of chess as actually played to the simplicity of the underlying system.

As an example of an early model of structural analysis, Ricoeur considers Vladimir Propp's work on the morphology of the Russian folktale. Propp's roots were in a Russian formalism that developed independently of Saussurean linguistics, but the attention bestowed on him by Lévi-Strauss and his influence on Barthes give him a significant place in the history of French structuralism. In Propp, we have someone very nearly resembling our imaginary observer at the chess tournament. Having examined a large number of Russian folktales, Propp isolated a limited number of elements—he called them "functions"—representing the equivalent of an underlying morphological system. Thus, for instance, the hero leaves home, the hero passes a test entitling him to a magical object or magical aid, an initial misfortune is resolved (a magic spell broken, a captive released), and so on. In the same way, Propp thought that every character in these tales—for instance, the "donor" who gives the hero a magical object, the "dispatcher" who sends the hero out on his quest—could be assigned to one of seven categories.

Ricoeur's point about Propp's analysis is that, like similar analyses proceeding on structuralist or semiotic assumptions—roughly, the search for an underlying "grammar" of narrative modes—it leaves out the teleological principle that gives meaning to the whole. This is difficult to see, not least because narrativity is so basic to our understanding of the world that we unconsciously supply the *telos*—that internal logic that connects one event to another within the story—when looking at something like Propp's table of narrative functions. But the *telos* is not *in* the table. Consider, once again, our imaginary chess tournament, except with, in the role of observer, a Martian anthropologist to whom even the most common forms of human activity are entirely unknown. In this situation, Ricoeur's point would be that a Martian might very well deduce and formalize the *rules* of chess by watching a sufficient number of matches, but would have no means of deducing the notion of "game"—and such related notions as "competing" and "wanting to win"—that makes chess a meaningful activity to earthlings.

As it happens, Propp was not unaware that something like a *telos* was missing from his narratological analysis. But he thought this lack could be overcome by expanding his segments to include what might be called linking actions. So, for instance, take a sequence like this: the hero leaves home, comes into possession of a magical object, redresses an original wrong—for instance, defeats the villain or fulfills a lack announced at the outset—then returns home and is transfigured (recognized as a hero). In formalizing such sequences, Propp uses a downward arrow "↓" to mark the point of the hero's return, corresponding to the upward arrow "↑" marking his departure. Put in this way, Propp seems to have redistributed something obviously recognizable as a quest narrative in structural terms, ones that have incorporated into the notion of "function" that *telos* of narrative development that moves the plot from the hero's departure to his return and transfiguration.

In the same way, Propp maintains that he has found an authentic structural equivalent to the *telos* of plot in his initial definition of character types—for example, the villain, the donor, the helper, the dispatcher—in terms of their spheres of action, much as, in chess, the relative spheres of action of pawn, knight, and bishop impose themselves on all actual chess openings. Yet this is, says Ricoeur, illusory. Propp himself, he notes, calls the development from one function to another within the tale a "move," such that a new instance of villainy, for example, generates a new series of functions. What this implicitly recognizes is that any such notion as "quest" implies a range of goals, purposes, and desires not reducible to outward action. This is why Propp's "algebraic rewriting" of functions and sequences, as Ricoeur calls it, would never be mistaken for an actual tale told by one person to others, any more than a systematic cataloguing of opening or endgame combinations would be mistaken for an actual game of chess.

Another crucial point, to stay with this example, is that "game" is, among other things, an irreducibly temporal concept. Just as we could not meaningfully ask someone to imagine a spatial object like a table outside space, we could not ask him to imagine a game of chess played outside of time. The result, as Wittgenstein pointed out in a related context, could only be a certain kind of significant nonsense. This is precisely Ricoeur's point about plot, which, since Aristotle's discussion of *mythos* in the *Poetics*, has always been understood as something that, although it may lend itself to ex post facto spatial representation, is primarily and irreducibly a sequence of events that unfold over time. What Propp is doing, therefore, is borrowing from the logic of Aristotelian *mythos*—the actual dynamics of narrative emplotment—various features that he then mistakenly supposes to be present in his initial system of structural constraints. What is absent is emplotment as the *telos* of narrative causality as it occurs in narrative time.

The same is true of the best known of the semiotic systems Ricoeur considers, the narratological analysis of Greimas. Here, the silent incorporation of a teleological element is harder to trace, not least because Greimas, a contemporary of Lévi-Strauss and Barthes, is working at the higher level of structural analysis suggested by Saussurean linguistics. So, for instance, Greimas invokes a set of "transformational rules" meant to generate narrative structures on the basis of a contract that is established, violated, and restored. Greimas's famous "semiotic square" (*carré semiotique*), with its relations of contrarity, contradiction, and presupposition, might, it is true, be taken as an attempt to reduce narrative to a "spatial" unfolding of possibilities already implicit in an initial set of constraints. Still, Greimas might plausibly claim even here to have accounted for any contingently temporal element, just as any sentence I might now utter could be shown to have been already implicit in the grammatical system and vocabulary that made my utterance possible.

Greimas's system begins from the notion of an *actant*: not an actual character, but the formal function that any character may fulfill in a narrative structure. The inspiration is clearly linguistic, "actant" being a narratological concept roughly equivalent to "noun" in grammar, not the specification of a word—for example, *run, laugh, jump*—but the function of the word in a sentence. (Consider "she had a run in her stocking" versus "see George run.") Greimas's first move is to isolate six actantial categories: A *desires* B (e.g., the hero sets out in search of someone); an act of *communication* relates A to B (e.g., the king charges the hero with a mission); or there is a *pragmatic* relation between A and B (e.g., B is either a helper or an opponent). So the basis of actantial roles is desire, communication, and action, each derived from an underlying binary opposition. The aim of Greimas's transformational rules is to set in motion the actantial categories—much as generative grammar displays the "hidden" transformation of active to passive sentences by appealing to rules of deep structure—by isolating "the test" (*l'épreuve*) through which the violated contract will or will not be restored.

Still, Ricoeur argues, all that Greimas has really done is redescribe the "quest" of Propp's hero in terms that he supposes to be purely synchronic or atemporal. What is missing, as before, is the *telos* without which a plot is not yet a plot. To see the point of Ricoeur's critique, imagine two people playing the child's game scissors-stone-paper. In semiotic terms, what matters is that the possibilities of any actual game can be laid out beforehand, such that a formal table of combinations, constructed on purely logical or mathematical grounds, seems to have mapped out in advance everything that occurs: scissors do cut paper (victory in a round), paper wraps stone (another victory), and so forth. In Greimas's system, this is the role of the semiotic square, which he imagines to have set out in advance the deep structure of actual narrative sequences.

What is actually going on, says Ricoeur, is something quite different. Consider: when I formalize the mathematical possibilities of scissors-stone-paper, the idea of a *game* is not part of the formalization. We are now in something like the situation of the chess tournament that we took as an analogy to Propp's morphology of folktales, except that here we are in a position to see more clearly the *telos* that keeps getting left out of structuralist analyses. For in both chess and scissors-stone-paper, it is such "game concepts" as competing or wanting to win that impose a teleological framework on the action: my "goal" or "end" or "purpose" is to win the contest, and this is *in principle* something that cannot be captured in a representation of formal constraints. In this sense, what gets left out by semiotic analysis is not just the *telos* of a plot, but any conception of characters in narrative—as opposed to "functions" or "actants"—as dwelling, like those of us in ordinary life, in a world of goals and purposes.

Among structuralist analyses of narrative, Ricoeur sees Claude Bremond's *Logique du récit* as having come closest to returning character to that sphere of volition and action from which the *telos* of plot derives. Curiously, it was not any sense of a missing teleology, but what he saw as a different limitation of Propp's system, that moved Bremond to attempt an alternative formulation. His argument was that Propp had mixed up logical considerations—those legitimately belonging to structural analysis—with others that were merely and contingently cultural. So, for instance, Propp's sequencing of functions always ends with the victory of the hero and punishment of the villain. But, as Bremond points out, no story need end with the hero's victory. The notion that victory implies struggle is a purely logical idea, and it may therefore be taken as an invariant structural principle. But the notion that struggle implies victory is culturally determined. Thus, Bremond set about constructing a logically adequate system of formal constraints by substituting characters for Propp's functions.

For Ricoeur, the great advance of Bremond's alternative system is not simply that it transforms Propp's functions into characters, but that it conceives characters as *persons*, thus bringing to light a semantics of action—goals, circumstances, interactions—that underlies the principle of emplotment in Aristotle's sense. Bremond begins by reducing plot to a table of phases: first possibility (Tom wants to marry Jane), then passage to the act (Tom proposes marriage) versus no passage (Jane's father forbids the match), and then completion (the couple gets married) versus noncompletion (the heroine dies). Bremond's taxonomy of characters begins from a simple dichotomy: a character in a story is at any given point a *sufferer*—one who is "affected by the events as narrated"—or an *agent*, one who sets events in motion. (*Sufferer* also includes characters affected by events no one has set in motion, such as a tornado, a car crash, cancer.) Such a scheme, says Bremond, preserves both "progressive contingency" (what will happen?) and "retroactive necessity" (yes, it was inevitable).

Even at this point, however, Ricoeur sees Bremond as having failed to account for emplotment as *telos*. As he says, knowing in advance all the roles capable of being assumed by characters—the ultimate aim, after all, of any properly structuralist analysis—"*is not yet to know any plot whatsoever*" ("*ce n'est encore connaître aucune intrigue*").[6] Like Propp before him, and like Greimas, Bremond has been unconsciously drawing on a logic of narrativity that lies outside the limits of his own system. Bremond's real contribution, in Ricoeur's eyes, was to have expanded structural analysis to include the possibility of ethical judgment, as when an agent gives a sufferer true or false information, or good or bad advice, which when acted on can ameliorate or worsen the sufferer's situation. Here, as Ricoeur points out, we are suddenly in the realm of *evaluations*: the wise counselor or the evil counselor is subject to evaluation in purely "intrinsic" terms according to the motive and consequences of his actions. This is a point that will be important when Ricoeur considers the relation of narrators to the stories they are telling.

Ricoeur's example of structural analysis that avoids the pitfall of excluding *telos* is the work of Northrop Frye, especially his *Anatomy of Criticism*. Since Frye's account of emplotment, like Ricoeur's own, derives from Aristotle, this is not entirely surprising. But Ricoeur, acutely aware of the limitations of French structuralism, may also have been drawn by the way the *Anatomy* manages to achieve many of the same results while treating literary structure in an intuitive, almost commonsensical way, without a great deal of elaborate theoretical machinery. Here, for instance, is Frye's account of plot in dramatic comedy:

What normally happens is that a young man wants a young woman, that his desire is resisted by some opposition, usually paternal, and that near the end of the play some twist in the plot enables the hero to have his will. In this simple pattern there are several complex elements. In the first place, the movement of comedy is usually a movement from one kind of society to another. At beginning of the play the obstructing characters are in charge of the play's society, and the audience recognizes that they are usurpers. At the end of the play the device in the plot that brings hero and heroine together causes a new society to crystallize around the hero, and the moment when this crystallization occurs is the point of resolution in the action, the comic discovery, *anagnorisis* or *cognitio*.[7]

Frye is describing the *mythos* of innumerable dramatic comedies, from Greek New Comedy to Hollywood romantic comedies produced in our own time. But what gives his brief summary analytic substance is its notion of an irresistible movement from a usurping society to a desirable society—that is, from a repressive social order based on money and power to an opposing order based on spontaneous or natural sympathies, for which the romantic attraction between hero and heroine serves as both emblem and catalyst of the plot. So, for instance, Frye points out that the blocking characters—the heroine's father, say, or the rich and usually repulsive young man he wants her to marry, or the crabbed guardian to whom a father's will has given power to withhold assent—are identified not simply with money and institutional power, but with an instinctive antipathy to the youth and spontaneity represented by the two lovers. Thus, something very like Greimas's notion of a "contract" is implicit in Frye's usurping society, the violated contract being, in this case, with certain perennial laws of natural attraction.

As with Aristotle's account of *mythos* in tragedy, Frye's account of comic plot in drama gives us a *telos* internal to the sequence of events in the play. Ethical or moral evaluations in this situation resemble Bremond's "intrinsic" judgments made in relation to actions affecting the principal characters, as with the evil counselor who intentionally misleads, and therefore causes suffering to, the hero and others. The moral perspective involved is something very like a Kantian universalism—for instance, the notion that anyone in any society understands what it would be like to be lied to, and then harmed or brought to ruin by that lie—which is what Frye means by saying that, in the case of comedy, the audience immediately understands those in the usurping society to represent an order of illegitimate power or authority. In drama, this moral perspective is then closely related to the perspective of the *totum simul*, or events suddenly perceived "as a whole," which is revealed in the moment of *anagnorisis*.

In what Aristotle called diegetic narrative, on the other hand—a story told to an audience by a storyteller, as opposed to a direct representation of events—the *totum simul* is, as we saw in chapter 1, always implied by the perspective of a narrator to whom the outcome of events is known before he or she begins telling the story. For Ricoeur, this is the single most important implication of Weinrich's account of the "narrative past"—the narrative use of the family of preterite verbs, indicating that the action being described took place at an earlier time—as a formal announcement, when employed in fictional narrative, that the reader or listener is about to enter an imaginary world. This is why, as we saw, Dickens's "It was the best of times, it was the worst of times," even when introducing a story set in the French Revolution, must be taken to abolish any relation to an actual past, signaling an ontological break between the world of Charles Darnay and Sydney Carton and the world of any actual reader of *A Tale of Two Cities*.

The space in which narrative unfolds, Weinrich memorably said, is not the past, by which he meant not only that narrative gives us an imaginary world, but that events and characters within that world exist in a temporal medium belonging to narrative alone. Here begins Ricoeur's theory of narrative as embodying a "third time," which corresponds neither to Aristotle's "time of the world" nor to the phenomenological time in which Augustine and Husserl sought an alternative to Aristotle's motion of the stars and the planets. For Ricoeur, the possibility of this third time can be seen to emerge from two closely related aspects of narrative structure: (1) an internal disproportion between the time of narration and the duration of events in the story, and (2) a teleological movement or forward-straining tension that develops as a purely formal consequence of that internal disproportion. Temporality matters, in short, because it is the medium without which there could be no *telos* of emplotment.

Time and Narrative draws substantially at this point on Günther Müller's analysis of the relation between *erzählte Zeit* (time taken by events narrated) and *Erzählzeit* (time of narration), which may for our purposes be taken as a temporal equivalent of the standard narratological distinction between story and discourse. In narratology, as Jonathan Culler succinctly puts it, *story* is conceived as "a nondiscursive, nontextual given, something which exists prior to and independently of narrative presentation." The point of the distinction is that these exist as separate orders of reality *within* any narrative structure:

> narratological analysis of a text requires one to treat the discourse as a representation of events which are conceived of as independent of any particular narrative perspective or presentation and which are thought of as having the properties of real events. Thus a novel may not identify the temporal relations between two events it presents, but the analyst must assume that there is a real or proper temporal order, that the events in fact occurred either simultaneously or successively.[8]

This is the framework within which Müller undertakes his analysis of the relation between *Erzählzeit* and *erzählte Zeit*. *Erzählte Zeit* might in this context be translated literally as "told time"—that is, the time actually taken up, as measured by clocks and calendars, by the events being recounted—and *Erzählzeit* as "telling time," or the time it takes to retell the same events as a story. The focus of Müller's analysis is on the variable relation these have to each other within narrative structure. This is not simply a literary matter—as when, say, a short story that can be read in twenty or thirty minutes covers events that took three years— but a feature of narrative structure at every level. The actual episode of my spouse's agonizing wait to get medical attention at the emergency room last week may have taken up three or four hours, but the telling of it, though leaving out no essential detail and conveying a full sense of her anguish and my own, may take only ten minutes. What necessarily emerges from the disproportion is a structure of significance.

The transmutation of *erzählte Zeit* into *Erzählzeit* involves a great deal more than a process of selection and ellipsis. At the level of narration, events that took a considerable amount of chronological time may be compressed into a sentence—"We sat there for over four hours, nobody paying any attention to us"—so as to shift the emphasis toward an interior or psychological time unmeasurable by clocks. Conversely, occurrences that took almost no time—"when I finally went up to the orderly, he just stood there with his hands on his hips, glaring at me, like he was too important to answer questions"—may expand to occupy major space in the narration, signaling an order of significance that has already begun to operate independent of objective time. Müller calls this process of transmutation *Raffung*, which may be translated as "pleating" or "folding." For Ricoeur, its primary importance is that it represents a break or rupture with linear time, a transformation of Aristotle's cosmic time into a time of human preoccupation or concern.

Here we encounter the reason that Ricoeur sees narrative time as the privileged medium of *telos* in plot. When narrative time has become predominantly a time of concern, moral or ethical significance will normally come to override bare succession—that is, events occurring in mere temporal sequence—in the narrated world. When it has done so, *telos* develops as the result of a tension between two narrative levels. At the level of events—the "story" of the narratologists, Müller's *erzählte Zeit*—characters move forward in a world where choices must be made with only an approximate guess about their consequences, where accidents might occur at any moment to alter the fortunes of the individual or the community, and where people must be judged on the shifting and uncertain ground of social appearances. At the level of narration, on the other hand, the story already exists as a completed whole—outcome known, motives weighed, characters judged—in the *totum simul* perspective of the narrator.

This brings into view a narrative time—or, better, a time of narration—that carries within itself two states of knowledge or awareness, while at the same time projecting a reader or listener drawn forward by continuous intimations that these are alternative versions of the same story. For Ricoeur, the explanation of plot as a teleological movement lies here. The temporal structure of narrative gives us a situation in which characters are moving forward in a state of partial or imperfect knowledge—Elizabeth and Darcy, say, as they proceed through a long series of misunderstandings and willful misprisions in *Pride and Prejudice*—that runs parallel to that of the reader. The crucial difference is that the reader is always conscious of viewing events through the eyes of a narrator who, knowing the story as a whole, is already viewing them in terms of their outcome, and who is viewing that outcome as an order of moral or ethical significance. *Telos* thus becomes a movement toward that moment of *anagnorisis* or recognition when those following the story will have revealed to them what the narrator has known from the outset.

In *Pride and Prejudice*, for instance, the story will end with the crystallization of something like Frye's desirable society—here, a "community of sense" that will exclude foolish or self-centered characters like Mrs. Bennet and Mr. Collins—around the united figures of heroine and hero. Ricoeur's point would be that this society already in some sense exists as an invisible or as-yet-to-be-realized ideal as events move forward, as is evident whenever the narrator's focus on Elizabeth and Darcy singles them out, in effect, as the couple who will be the center of the community of sense that emerges at the end. Consider the dinner party where the egregious Mrs. Bennet is loudly congratulating herself because she supposes the wealthy young Mr. Bingley to be on the point of proposing marriage to her eldest daughter Jane:

> In vain did Elizabeth endeavour to check the rapidity of her mother's words, or persuade her to describe her felicity in a less audible whisper; for to her inexpressible vexation, she could perceive that the chief of it was overheard by Mr. Darcy, who sat opposite to them. Her mother only scolded her for being nonsensical.
>
> "What is Mr. Darcy to me, pray, that I should be afraid of him? I am sure we owe him no such particular civility as to be obliged to say nothing *he* may not like to hear." . . .
>
> Nothing that she could say, however, had any influence. Her mother would talk of her views in the same intelligible tone. Elizabeth blushed and blushed again with shame and vexation. She could not help frequently glancing her eye at Mr. Darcy, though every

glance convinced her of what she dreaded; for though he was not always looking at her mother, she was convinced that his attention was invariably fixed by her. The expression of his face changed gradually from indignant contempt to a composed and steady gravity.[9]

In any such episode we see readily enough why Ricoeur, having exposed the limitations of the structuralist analyses of Propp and Greimas, is drawn to Frye's mode of analysis in *The Anatomy of Criticism*. For Frye, like Ricoeur, conceives of narrative time as an ethical as well as a temporal medium, and of the *telos* of emplotment as comprehensible only when viewed in ethical as well as temporal terms. Thus we have, in the dinner party scene, strong intimations of the narrator's shared sense of Elizabeth's emotional anguish—"Elizabeth blushed again and again with shame and vexation"—and of a movement that is already working to exclude characters like her mother from the community of sense. This logic of emplotment, Ricoeur would argue, is one that demands seeing all parties to the transaction—Elizabeth, Darcy, the narrator, the reader—as dwelling in a realm of volition, will, and action that implies the possession of a moral consciousness. This is what was missing from the "functions" of Propp's narrative grammar and the "actants" of Greimas's semiotic analysis.

In *Pride and Prejudice*, the movement toward Frye's desirable society thus involves a winnowing out of the foolish or irretrievably self-interested characters—Sir William Lucas, Mr. Collins, Mr. Wickham, Lady Catherine de Bourgh, the Bingley sisters, Elizabeth's own younger sisters, their aunt Philips—until only members of the community of sense remain—Elizabeth, Darcy, Jane, Bingley, Elizabeth's aunt and uncle Gardiner, and even Mr. Bennet himself, on the way to recovery from a misanthropic pessimism. For Ricoeur, as for Frye, this is not simply a result of the *telos* of plot. It is the *telos* itself. In ethical terms, its power of clarification comes from permitting the reader to see that foolishness and wickedness—the failings of characters as otherwise dissimilar as, say, Mr. Collins and Wickham—are simply different forms of an identical egoism that blinds one to the moral claim of others to be treated as persons. It is through this clarification that the notion of sense in Austen assumes a nearly Kantian dimension.

To translate what Elizabeth and Darcy come to learn into Kantian terms, however—that is, into a maxim within an abstract system of ethics—would be to miss an important part of Ricoeur's argument in *Time and Narrative*. For at the heart of that argument lies a conception of narrative time as a mode of moral experience, the privileged domain of what Henry James, in a discussion of novels and novelists, once calls the moral imagination. Ricoeur's account of the *telos* of emplotment is meant to explain why *Pride and Prejudice* invites the reader to accompany Elizabeth and Darcy in their own state of imperfect knowledge, and thus through their own purging of egoism, to the moment of *anagnorisis* when they come truly to understand each other, and themselves, for the first time. This is what Ricoeur will call the "third time" of narrative. It permits the reader to achieve *anagnorisis* at the same moment, and on the same terms, as the hero and heroine.

Ricoeur's deeper point will be that the *anagnorisis* of the reader conveys knowledge that cannot be meaningfully expressed in propositional terms. For him, this is also the point of Aristotle's description of catharsis in the *Poetics*, that purging of pity and fear brought about by accompanying Oedipus on his terrible journey to self-knowledge and then miraculously being able to walk away unharmed from the Athenian theater, or to finish the last page of *Oedipus Rex*, put down the book, and resume one's activities in ordinary life. The meaning of catharsis—and, as we shall see, the related process that Ricoeur calls "application"—is that there is an alteration of consciousness that must remain merely speculative when talked about propositionally—"losing a loved one is unbearably painful"—but that becomes indelibly real when actually experienced, as when one's spouse is killed in an accident or one's child dies of cancer. Only within the reality constructed by narrative is such experience possible without actual dread or harm or loss.

Here we encounter Ricoeur at his most Aristotelian, especially in relation to the concept of *mimēsis praxeōs* discussed in chapter 1. For at the end point of Ricoeur's theory of narrative lies the same notion of an "object of imitation"—a purely abstract movement from partial or imperfect knowledge to *anagnorisis* or recognition—that he originally brought to light by following Aristotle's logic of mimesis through to a conclusion that in the *Poetics* remains only implicit. The structure that

Aristotle located in Greek tragedy in general and Sophoclean tragedy in particular thus emerges in *Time and Narrative* as the core of a universal grammar of narrativity, one understood in every age and culture. And the epistemic gain of narrative experience, to borrow David Parker's phrase once again, emerges for Ricoeur as a alteration of consciousness akin to the alteration that he himself associates with his earlier work on metaphor, which he calls a radical power of reference to "those aspects of our being-in-the-world that cannot be talked about directly" ("les aspects de notre être-au-monde qui ne peuvent être dits de manière direct").[10]

In volume 2 of *Time and Narrative*, Ricoeur discusses three works—Virginia Woolf's *Mrs Dalloway*, Thomas Mann's *The Magic Mountain*, and Proust's *In Search of Lost Time*—which he sees as exploring, in their very telling, the strange nature of a temporality that is also a medium of moral or ethical experience. Of these three writers, Ricoeur thinks, Proust comes closest to expressing what he means here by the radical power of narrative to alter one's own way of being in the world. For Proust understands that this is in the end a power, not given to us on any other terms, simply to see as others do. Without art, says Proust, I could never understand how different my world is from yours, "a difference which, if there were no art, would remain forever the secret of every individual. Through art alone are we able to emerge from ourselves, to know what another person sees of a universe which is not the same as our own and of which, without art, the landscapes would remain as unknown to us as those that may exist on the moon."[11] For Ricoeur, as we shall see, this might be taken as the ultimate point of his own theory of time and narrative.

Chapter Four

SEMANTICS OF ACTION

TIME AND NARRATIVE TAKES AS ITS SUBJECT BOTH HISTORICAL
and fictional narrative: Jacques Le Goff's *Time, Work, and Culture in
the Middle Ages* along with Woolf's *Mrs Dalloway*, Fernand Braudel's
The Mediterranean along with Proust's *In Search of Lost Time*. Indeed, a
major part of Ricoeur's argument, as we shall see in chapter 5, will be devoted to showing that a work like Braudel's, which famously presented
itself as being history in a non-narrative or even anti-narrative mode,
appeals constantly to a logic of emplotment intelligible only in terms
of narrative causality. The basis of this peculiar sort of causality—that
internal relation between events that permits us to say that one thing
in a story happens, as Aristotle said, "because of" another—is, Ricoeur
wants us to see, nothing less than an "understanding immanent in the
order of action and . . . the prenarrative structures stemming from real
action."[1] This notion of causality is based on a teleology of human action: doing something to attain an end or fulfill a purpose. For Ricoeur,
the significance of narrative as a means of understanding the world
originates here.

Nonetheless, the notion of narrative causality remains problematic.
One major reason is wholly familiar: as Kant saw almost immediately,
Newton's *Principia* had signaled the beginning of an epoch in which
material or physical causality would come to seem the only coherent
concept available to enlightened minds. For what Newton had demon-
strated was that the laws of motion at work in the ordinary world—what

is sometimes called the billiard-ball notion of causality—were uniform throughout the physical universe, and were, into the bargain, both demonstrable and empirically verifiable. Against this background, the notion of mental causation—"he put out his hand because he wanted another sip of coffee"—could hardly seem anything more than the remnant of an archaic folk psychology, something that would one day be wholly explained in terms of neurological states and synaptic firings. Teleological explanation, by the same token—"he proposed marriage because he'd fallen in love with her"—could hardly be taken as anything more than an exercise in tautology.

On the other hand, there are cases in which nomological explanation—that is, scientific explanation in terms of lawlike generalizations—seems obviously useless in relation to the untidy heterogeneity of human circumstance. The reasoning that tells me that all samples of copper carbonate will be composed of five parts copper, four parts oxygen, and one part carbon, or that specimens of water will boil at 100 degrees Celsius, seems beside the point when I am trying to understand why my favorite Aunt Emma has just cut me out of her will, or why the mayor of my town has abruptly resigned without giving any explanation to the voters. Ricoeur's point will be that a causality rooted in volition and action stands in the same relation to social or cultural reality as material causality stands in relation to the physical universe. Furthermore, just as material causality derives its authority from nomological generalization, this alternative causality of motive and action can be shown to derive its authority from narrative, which is itself rooted in the prenarrative structure of real action.

This is the domain of a semantics of action, which involves understanding others in terms of their motives and intentions and beliefs. In *Time and Narrative*, Ricoeur discusses the subject primarily in connection with problems in historical interpretation. He does so not because he favors history over imaginative literature—indeed, as we shall see, he means his point about the "prenarrative structure of real action" to apply as much to fictional as to historical narrative—but because philosophers have mainly treated the problem of meaningful human action in relation to various theories of historical truth. The primary issue has tended to be whether history is, or can be, a "scientific" discipline.

One sees why. To understand why a rock falls, I clearly need nomological reasoning. To understand why John Wilkes Booth assassinated Abraham Lincoln, I obviously need another sort of reasoning. But to understand why America dropped the atomic bomb on Hiroshima— including understanding the physics that led to its design and, at another level, determining whether it makes any sense to talk about an entity called "America" here—I need to reason in a way that somehow combines elements of both.

In the immediate background of Ricoeur's own approach is Wilhelm Dilthey, who argued that historical explanation uses a mode of reasoning utterly distinct from that of the physical sciences. This is, famously, Dilthey's concept of *Verstehen*, which in German simply means "understanding," but which he adopted as a technical term for understanding what goes on in the minds of others. This—for example, what occurs when I know from your frown that I've just said something displeasing to you—is what Dilthey opposed to *Erklären*, or "explanation," meaning nomological reasoning in science. For Ricoeur, as for Heidegger and Weber before him, two points in Dilthey's thought have cardinal significance. The first is that every human being must be viewed as having been born into a world that is already meaningful, where people dwell within their culture as a complex system of values and beliefs. The second is that, within this culture, certain abstract structures—law, politics, religion, social hierarchy, and so forth—assume an autonomous power to mold or channel individual will and action. Dilthey himself called these *die Objektivationen des Lebens*, or "objectifications of life."

At the simplest level, the *Verstehen* principle seems to imply that we understand other people by looking directly into their minds. This is impossible in any literal sense, of course, but such understanding does seem to occur spontaneously when we know other people well within a shared cultural situation. I can tell when my friend is depressed without his having to say a word, and if I know enough about the circumstances— his recent divorce, say, from a spouse who was having an affair with someone else—I have a ready explanation of his mood and behavior. Similarly, the *Verstehen* principle is obviously at work when an anthropologist goes to live with a tribe whose culture he wants to grasp from the inside. This is the principle Dilthey saw as being the essential basis of historical explanation. If I want to understand why the Pilgrims set out for America, or why the French stormed the Bastille, or how the Nazis were able to sway large numbers of people in Weimar Germany, I must begin by attempting to think as they thought and see as they saw within their own cultural circumstances.

This is the basis of the theory set forth in in R. G. Collingwood's *The Idea of History*, where historical truth is taken to result from uncovering and reconstructing experience that is at an essential level like our own, but that took place in far different circumstances. What makes history radically different from the physical sciences, Collingwood argues, is that historical events have an "inside"—how the historical actors understood themselves and their actions—as well as an "outside," meaning a subjection to external forces such as climate, geography, social institutions, and the like. Collingwood's "outside" corresponds, it will be seen, to any social and physical environment independent of consciousness, and his "inside" to the thoughts and motives of human agents. The outside plays a major role in his theory—it is only within an external environment that thoughts can take shape as actions—and the inside includes a great deal more than rational calculation, as when unconscious desires or undeclared animosities become, along with conscious motives, a mainspring of action.

Sound historical reasoning thus results, on Collingwood's theory, in what he calls a reenactment of the past. The attractions of the theory are obvious. If I want to understand why the French stormed the Bastille, I will want to start by learning as much as possible, in the tradition of "objective" inquiry, about the economic state of France, the record of recent harvests, the system of taxation as it placed an unequal burden on rich and poor, the growth of Paris as an urban environment in which the extremes of wealth and poverty were exposed to daily view, the circulation of radical ideas among an educated class, and the like. But then I will also want to try my best to understand the thoughts and emotions of those who threw their bodies into the assault, and in particular the degree to which they might have understood themselves as actors in a symbolic episode with repercussions far beyond the immediate scene of action. This is historical explanation as *Verstehen*, something at which no examination of economic statistics or agricultural records, no matter how exhaustive, can ever arrive.

Still, there are serious problems with Collingwood's theory. The first is a purely epistemological objection. It is that no notion of "reenactment," even when it means, as it does for Collingwood, an imaginative replaying of the original event from the viewpoint of the actors, guarantees that one's own thoughts will be the same as theirs. So, for instance, I might exactly reenact for the police a bank robbery I have just witnessed, even entering through the same door, retracing the same steps, and standing in front of the same teller's cage as the robber. But none of this means that my thoughts will be the same as his. A second, deeper objection is that even when we have tried to put ourselves in the position of the original actors—here, when I try to imagine the robber's thoughts when walking through my reenactment—there is in principle no way for me to discover whether or not what I am imagining is in any way related to what he was actually thinking. This is the sense in which Collingwood's historical idealism, as Ricoeur says, leaves him face to face not with the past but with his own thoughts about the past.

At the opposite extreme from Collingwood are theories of history as a wholly objective discipline, the aim of which is usually to eliminate a "psychologism" incompatible with methodological rigor. The best-known example, found in Karl Hempel's landmark essay "The Function of General Laws in History," would subsequently become known, though Hempel himself did not call it that, as the covering law model of historical explanation. Hempel's idea was that a properly objective mode of historical inquiry might work in the same way that engineers explain singular events like the bursting of a dam, or geologists explain an earthquake or the eruption of a volcano. To be sure, there can be no question of exact prediction in such cases—prediction being the usual measure of scientific validity—but there are physical laws, and data available after the fact, and means of objectively reconstructing the event. The dam did burst, and had enough detailed data about concrete stress, water volume, and similar factors been available, the event in principle could have been predicted.

For a historian attempting to understand the French Revolution, the attractions of Hempel's covering law model are clear. In an age when the methods of quantitative history have become enormously sophisticated—for instance, that gathering and analysis of demographic, economic, epidemiological, and other statistics that enjoyed a brief popularity as "cliometrics"—the notion that a sufficiently detailed understanding of antecedent conditions might have permitted prediction of the event does not seem implausible. Here, knowledge about rapacious taxation, poor harvests, a growing inequality of wealth, and similar factors can seem very like a reconstruction based on concrete stress and water volume in the case of the dam. Like a dam that bursts, flooding the fields and drowning the villagers below, similarly, one might be tempted to say, the French men and women who stormed the Bastille released a torrent of social rage that would carry France through the execution of Louis XVI and the September massacres to Robespierre and the Terror, until, like floodwaters at last subsiding, a relative peace was restored by Napoleon's coup d'état of 18 Brumaire.

In Ricoeur's view, Hempel's covering law model is fundamentally but also instructively wrong. It is fundamentally wrong because it mistakes the very nature of historical explanation by introducing physical or material causality into a domain where an essential contingency deriving from human volition plays a major role. Ricoeur cites Charles Frankel, who argued against Hempel that the concept of a singular event in science—*this* earthquake, the bursting of *this* dam—and in history—the execution of Louis XVI, Hitler's reoccupation of the Rhineland—are utterly dissimilar. History, Frankel pointed out, deals with "individual events that have occurred once and only once."[2] Only an equivocation on the term "event" permits the covering law theorist to treat "revolution" as a recurrent phenomenon explicable in terms of a universal regularity. It is instructively wrong because Hempel's theory inspired various attempts to think through seriously the role of volition and contingency in history. In these, when their separate claims have been carefully weighed, Ricoeur sees the basis of a more fully developed semantics of action.

An important move in this direction was made, he thinks, by William H. Dray, who, in his *Laws and Explanations in History*, counterposed to Hempel's model a notion of singular explanation that is not explanation according to universal laws. The influence of Hempel's theory is decisive—Dray was, in fact, the first to call the theory the covering law model—because it has so obviously prompted drastic reconsideration of historical idealism like Collingwood's. Material or physical causality does play, Dray acknowledges, a necessary part in historical explanation, as it does in explaining events in ordinary life. Consider: my uncle was electrocuted when his radio fell into the bathtub. Any reasonable explanation of such an event will be *supported* by universal laws—here, those having to do with water and electricity—but what is also needed is a higher-order story about a sequence of events: the boy hit a ball through the window, it knocked the radio off its shelf, and so on. Historical inference then involves deciding which events do and which do not belong to this story.

The theory that Dray develops as an alternative to the covering law model begins in a rejection of Hempel's notion of historical causality. Hempel had seen, quite properly, that historians very often use expressions of the form "X causes Y": the French Revolution was caused by excessive taxation, economic exploitation, social inequality, and the like. But, being a philosopher of science—Dray never says this, but it is implicit in his argument—Hempel mistook this for the universalizing "if X, then Y" of nomological reasoning: if the temperature of H_2O is lowered below zero degrees Celsius, it will crystallize. What he failed to realize, argues Dray, is that the historian's "if X then Y" is something quite different, a rule of inference specifically meant to separate out contingent from necessary causes: if the French fleet had not arrived in time to provide naval support for Washington's troops, the Continental Army would not have won the Battle of Yorktown. This is a mode of explanation that assigns due weight to material causality—the wind and tides that permitted the French to arrive in time—but that also leaves ample room for contingency and human volition.

At this point, Dray is close to what Anglo-American philosophy calls counterfactual inference, a mode of reasoning that uses contrary-to-fact hypotheses—Ricoeur, following Raymond Aron, will call these "unreal constructions"—to test what is and what is not relevant to explanation. His point will be that historians automatically use such inference to rule out an indefinitely large class of "true" empirical facts that have no bearing on the event to be explained. ("The French Revolution would never have happened if Jacques Dupont, a *cordonnier* in Oullins, had not eaten oatmeal three days in a row.") Having thus eliminated all candidates for the role of cause whose absence would not have changed the course of events, the historian's "X caused Y" becomes a simple claim that *this* factor was necessary: "The assassination of the Archduke Ferdinand was a link in the causal chain leading to the outbreak of war." Obviously, a detailed knowledge of treaties, alliances, economic conditions, and the like will then be necessary to "explain" World War I. But none of this involves Hempel's covering laws.

Dray counterposes to Hempel's model a theory of what he calls rational explanation, meaning explanation in terms of an agent's reasons or calculations. He especially wants to preserve the genuine insight that led to Collingwood's historical idealism—"relive, reenact, rethink, are Collingwood's terms,"[3] says Ricoeur, endorsing Dray's aim—while avoiding the danger of dissolving into mere psychologism. What is needed, says Dray, is "a *logical* analysis of explanation," the grounds for which he finds in an agent's calculation when acting.[4] This is not deductive reasoning. It involves positing the sort of explanation someone might have given after acting in a certain way—"I threw water on the fire because I wanted to put it out"—and includes unpremeditated actions that had unintended consequences. ("No, I had no idea the bucket was filled with kerosene.") We move, here, away from theories of historical explanation and toward that semantics of action that Ricoeur sees as being central to understanding both historical and fictional narrative.

Dray's theory of rational explanation also sheds light on what Aristotle meant by the probability of an action. For Dray's model demands what he calls a logical equilibrium between reasons and actions, as when my belief that water puts out fire may be taken to explain why I ran to get a bucket. Dray's formulation is as follows: "if *y* is a good reason for A to do *x*, then *y* would be a good reason for anyone sufficiently like A to do *x* under sufficiently similar circumstances."[5] There is a danger that Dray's "sufficiently like" and "sufficiently similar" might be taken as circular, a way of setting things up so that counterexamples can be unfairly ruled out of court in advance. But the danger is less than it appears. Dray's point is that the notion of logical equilibrium in itself demands a specific understanding of any given set of circumstances. (A member of a tribe that knew nothing about buckets might not, for instance, grasp the use of the galvanized metal object lying nearby.) In somewhat different terms, Ricoeur observes, this is just the point Aristotle means to make in the *Poetics* when discussing his notion of the probable.

At the level of individual behavior, Ricoeur thinks, Dray's theory has much to recommend it. It seems clear to him, especially, that the notion of logical equilibrium plays an important role whenever we are trying to understand the actions of others. Yet he also thinks that Dray's theory is severely limited, for it provides no way to account for what Ricoeur calls "nonindividual social forces." He is thinking not merely of impersonal forces such as economic or technological change, but also of social forces like nationality and religion. What are we to do, for instance, with a statement like—the example is Dray's own—"Germany invaded Russia in 1941 because it feared a Russian attack from the rear"? Dray's idea is that "Germany" might be taken as a kind of surrogate individual, through reference to those with authority to act for the nation. But this would be, as Ricoeur points out, to take "Germany" as representing a sum of individual intentions, which would then be to understand history itself as nothing more than a "sum of individual processes analyzed in intentional terms."[6] This is, for him, the fatal weakness of Dray's theory.

The sense of a stark opposition between Dilthey's *Erklären* and *Verstehen* is very strong at this point in Ricoeur's argument. Though Hempel's attempt to apply laws of material causality to a reality partly governed by human volition was in some obvious sense misguided, it was not altogether wrong. Natural cataclysms do change the course of events. Technological developments do alter human societies. Economic conditions are determined by forces outside human control. On the other hand, theories of human action such as Dray's, dealing with motives, intentions, beliefs, and rational calculation, are just as obviously necessary to get at the heterogeneity of historical experience. The Rubicon, considered simply as a geographical feature of the Italian landscape, is a physical fact. The decision of the Roman Senate to order Caesar and his legions to remain on its far side is an institutional fact. Caesar's decision to cross over and march on Rome is a fact about human volition. The problem for historical explanation is to bring these into an intelligible relation.

The great value of theories like Dray's, as Ricoeur sees it, is that they allow us to perceive more clearly how our ordinary understanding of human action—what Dilthey's *Verstehen* represents mainly in terms of an unexplained "intuition"—actually operates. This is especially

true of the theory Ricoeur considers as a more satisfactory alternative to what he calls Dray's methodological individualism, namely, the
"mixed" causal analysis of G. H. von Wright. Here, once again, Ricoeur
is ostensibly concerned with historical explanation. But, as always, he is
quite as much concerned with the general problem of heterogeneity in
human action, those interactions between consciousness and material
circumstances that, for most of us most of the time, constitute the stuff
of daily existence. In von Wright's model, which shows in detail how
volition can be integrated into a causal chain without being reduced to a
mere behavioral reflex, Ricoeur thinks we are given something like that
prenarrative understanding of action in which narrative is ultimately
rooted.

Consider, for instance, what is involved in any perfectly ordinary
action, as when we see a neighbor come out of his house to mow his
lawn. To anyone living in an American suburb—houses, lawns, power
mowers—what happens next is self-explanatory. To grasp the essentials
of von Wright's theory, however, or to see why Ricoeur wants to make
considerable claims for its explanatory power, it is useful to imagine
how the same combination of actions and circumstances might look
to someone who knew nothing about our neighbor's form of life. Von
Wright's analysis begins with the way the world is now being perceived
by the neighbor, which is as a set of logically independent states of
affairs—the sun is shining, the grass is five inches high, the mower is
filled with gas—within which his action is to take place. The crucial
point for von Wright is that the neighbor has already constituted what
might be called a world-within-a-world—thinking specifically of Wittgenstein's logical atomism in the *Tractatus*, von Wright calls this a "frag-
ment of the world"—as a context of meaningful action.

Imagine now that our neighbor pulls the cord to start the engine
of his mower. At this stage, all that von Wright's analysis demands is
an elementary sequence that can be formalized as pTq, which means
that p happened, THEN q happened: the neighbor pulled the cord, then
the engine started. For all its simplicity, this is a powerful move in the
direction of integrating volition into what would otherwise be a chain
of purely material causes. The mower, after all, is subject entirely to
physical laws, which here involve the mechanics of internal combustion.

Considered purely as a physical event, pulling the cord is covered by the same laws. But now von Wright has redescribed the sequence in terms of a movement from one state of affairs to another—the change that has occurred when the engine starts up—in a way that leaves only a volitional act as a candidate for explaining the causal link between the two. This exposes the "internal" link between states A and B, or the structure of what von Wright calls a basic action.

An expanded version of the same model then allows von Wright to account for the internal relation between basic actions and more distant states of affairs. His emphasis, once again, is on the way an agent isolates "fragments of the world"—here, the fact that the grass is five inches high will be added to the states of affairs our neighbor is considering, though to a visitor who knew nothing about lawns and mowers, the relation of this fact to pulling a cord might not be evident—and makes the action explicable in terms of a controlling intention. The key concept at this point becomes what Ricoeur calls an intervention.[7] At the level of basic action, pulling the starter cord counts as an intervention, for in a world without volition and intention, the mower might well have sat motionless until it rusted away. Von Wright's terminology for this is that there is a state α such that it would not, without intervention, change to state a. Here Ricoeur sees the basis of a more comprehensive semantics of action.

Von Wright's concept of a basic action is borrowed from Arthur Danto. There is, to give von Wright's own formulation, "a state α such that we feel confident, on the basis of past experience, that α *will not change* to a state a, unless *we change it* to a. And assume this is something (we know) *we can do*."[8] Then, to move from a basic action to more distant states of affairs—to get, so to speak, from the pulling of the starter cord to the mowed lawn—he also takes over Danto's notion of a result, which is intended to account for the logical structure of a volitional act. The main distinction, as Danto himself says, is between doing something and "bringing something about (by doing something else)." Von Wright calls this a mixed mode of explanation. It is causal (the mower started because the spark plug fired) and at the same time teleological (the sequence ending with the mowed lawn can only be accounted for in terms of an aim or intention). This is, in short, action intentionalistically understood: "To bring about *p* I must do *x*; I wish to bring about *p*; therefore, I must do *x*."[9]

Von Wright's concern is with historical explanation, but for Ricoeur a crucial point about this practical syllogism is that it lays bare a teleological structure that explains the basis of narrative causality. In emplotment, we recall Aristotle saying, one thing happens "because of" another, but he had no explanation for the "internal" relation between events assumed by his observation. Now, with von Wright, we have a structure that in one direction leads from intention to result—the "idea of a reason for acting" discussed earlier—and does so, moreover, whether or not that result occurs. (My pulling the starter cord must be, in von Wright's terminology, "intentionalistically appreciated" *as* an action even if I am called to the phone and never get back to actually mowing the lawn.) Read in reverse, on the other hand—that is, from result to original action—we have a sequence that can only be explained teleologically. The lawn has been mowed, and every intermediate step in the chain of events must be understood as having been subject to a controlling intention.

Two factors in von Wright's analysis are especially important to Ricoeur. The first is that the "T" of von Wright's pTq introduces a temporality needed for teleological understanding. For von Wright himself, T is simply the atemporal marker of logical entailment, similar to the *then* of "if A, then B." But in a theory of action—this is what Ricoeur sees, and takes over into his own theory—A can only follow B in time: "he pulled the cord, *then* the mower started." This temporality is what Ricoeur might have called a "time of volition." The second feature is that in von Wright's analysis, the *telos* of intention dominates or controls external circumstances. This explains how Aristotle's "grasping together" of heterogeneous elements in narrative actually occurs. Consider: I pull the cord and my mower doesn't start. I can borrow a neighbor's. If my neighbor isn't home, I can go to a rental company. If I am frustrated enough, I can buy a new mower. But through this shifting series of circumstances, everything—if one wants to explain the mowed lawn that finally does result—must be brought into an intelligible relation with the intention that has been ordering events from beginning to end.

We are now in a position to see why Ricoeur, whose ostensible concern is with narrative, has devoted so much time to the semantics of action. For what von Wright has done is to fill in a crucial missing step in Aristotle's theory of narrative as *mimēsis praxeōs*, the imitation of an action. Aristotle attributed narrative causality, that *telos* that induces us to see one thing happening "because of" another, entirely to a structure imposed on events by the storyteller. What von Wright brings to view, on the other hand, is a teleological structure *within* human action that is simply taken over into emplotment. Even ordinary actions, he has shown, are intelligible only in terms of a controlling intention that brings into play volition, motive, belief, and a specific estimate of external circumstances. So, insofar as emplotment incorporates into itself the action of conscious agents—of Oedipus, or Hamlet, or Satan in *Paradise Lost*—plot will itself be teleological, and narrative causality will be a version of that "internal" relation between otherwise unrelated states of affairs posited by von Wright's analysis.

Still, Aristotle made a distinction between *poiēsis*, or imaginative writing, in which he saw a logic of emplotment clearly in evidence, and history, which he tended to view as a rendering of unconnected events. Ricoeur, on the other hand, will insist that history is an irreducibly narrative mode, not least because, in taking human action as its subject, it cannot avoid incorporating into itself the teleological structure of real action. At a certain level of conventional or traditional history, this presents no problems. When we ask why Caesar chose to cross the Rubicon, for instance, or what aim Hitler had in mind when he ordered German troops to reoccupy the Rhineland, we are clearly dealing with something very like the semantics of action analyzed by von Wright in terms of basic actions and more distant states of affairs. Such actions occur in a collective context, to be sure—we must take into account the legions who followed Caesar to Rome, the German nation that was launched on a tide of war and conquest by Hitler's decision—but at their center stands a volitional act analyzable in the same terms as ordinary actions.

What, then, are we to make of those larger entities—the Roman republic, the German nation—that undergo drastic change due to the volitional act of a Caesar or a Hitler? This was precisely the problem, we recall, that led Ricoeur to set aside Dray's theory of logical equilibrium, which made a great deal of sense at the level of individual action but which could do no more with a concept like "Germany"—in a historical statement such as "Germany feared an attack from the rear by

Russia"—than to imagine it as a kind of super-agent composed of the individual wills of millions of individual Germans. The difficulties are obvious. When Hitler reoccupied the Rhineland, there were many Germans who disapproved of his decision on moral grounds, millions more who, with the horror and carnage of World War I fresh in their minds, felt nothing but dread, and still others, incited by Nazi protestations of wounded national honor, who greeted the news with transports of joy. "Germany" is, in such a case, an abstraction that obviously falls far short of a complex historical reality.

This particular objection matters greatly to Ricoeur, not least because it threatens his conception of history as an irreducibly narrative mode. For historical explanation does normally feature statements that cast collective entities in the role of individual actors: "Germany bitterly resented the provisions of the Versailles Treaty," "Germany secretly rearmed during the 1920s, preparing the way for Hitler's militarism in the 1930s," and so on. The nominalist view that such abstractions stand for nothing at all, that they are simply empty names used to simplify a more complex historical reality, is already a serious challenge to such statements. To Ricoeur, however, the same objection represents an additional challenge. It is that his theory of history as narrative demands that "Germany" in such cases be treated as an actual actor—what he will call a "quasi-character"—at the level of historical events, with a claim to reality rooted in the social existence of actual human beings.

The basis of this claim becomes clearer if we note that "Hitler" and "Germany" in our earlier statements were used as nearly interchangeable terms. Hitler did not reoccupy the Rhineland—a single individual could scarcely do that—nor did "Germany," a nation of millions, most of whom were at home or at work when thirty thousand German troops marched across the bridges in 1936. What gives such terms meaning is that they refer to concepts—family, tribe, clan, nation—that are *constitutive* of individual consciousness, and which therefore have a real existence in what Husserl called the *Lebenswelt* or "life world" of men and women. We are very close here to those "objectifications of life" that Dilthey said must be assigned an autonomous role in historical explanation, especially when our goal is to understand individuals in history the way they understood themselves. To understand why the Pilgrims set out for America, it is necessary to understand Calvinism not merely as a theology but as a psychic or spiritual force in the *Lebenswelt* of those who were persecuted as Calvinists.

What, then, might be meant by "Germany" when we are talking about the reoccupation of the Rhineland? Ricoeur takes from Maurice Mandelbaum a working definition of "society" as used in historical contexts: a group that occupies a given territory, has institutions that assign roles to individuals, and perpetuates itself by assigning them these roles. Taken together, Ricoeur argues, these factors generate "an ethics of participatory belonging," meaning that individuals understand themselves not only as belonging to a group—as, say, one might join a club from which one is free to resign—but as sharing a common destiny. So, for instance, I buy land and build a house with a sense that my nation "occupies a territory" in which my rights of ownership are ultimately rooted. I work as a bank manager or worship as a Presbyterian with a sense that my role in the community is being sustained by institutions separate from my personal identity. This is the category of what Ricoeur will call first-order entities, meaning that they are directly rooted in the real life of men and women.

Any first-order entity, Ricoeur thinks, may legitimately be treated as a quasi-character (*quasi-personnage*) in historical narrative. The prefix *quasi* belongs to a vocabulary that Ricoeur uses throughout—he will speak, along with quasi-character, of quasi-event and quasi-plot—and in English can be taken to imply that what it precedes is somehow incomplete or unreal. This is not Ricoeur's meaning. If Ricoeur were to say that "Germany" functions as a quasi-character in "Germany reoccupied the Rhineland," he would mean that, along with a specific body of German troops, an entity called "Germany" really did reoccupy the Rhineland, and was universally understood to have done so. The point is that such entities have a semi-autonomous status in historical reality. To say that "America suffered during the Great Depression" is not to imply that "America" may be dissolved into individuals all of whom suffered during the 1930s. Indeed, some may have come out of that decade wealthier than before. What is meant is that an ethics of participatory belonging justifies treating "America" as a social whole within which a sense of economic crisis was universally shared.

The implications for a theory of narrative are considerable. As soon as "Hitler" is understood to represent something more than a mere individual—"Hitler reoccupied the Rhineland to test the will of the Allies to resist German expansion"—we have an action that becomes immediately intelligible in terms of von Wright's model, as a volitional act that explains the "inner" connection between successive states of affairs. This is not to say that Ricoeur wants to convert the episode into a story about volition and action only. To the contrary, he fully recognizes that the historian will need a great deal of empirical evidence—about German armaments production, about the relative size of the French and German armies, about the current economic situation in Europe, and a great deal more—to set Hitler's decision in context. But Ricoeur does see the episode as fully intelligible only as a story in which millions of people were seeing their own fates as deeply involved in those of "Germany" or "Poland" or "America" as actors on the stage of world history.

What becomes, then, of Aristotle's distinction between *poiēsis* and historical writing—between, say, *Oedipus Rex* or the *Odyssey* and Herodotus's episodic chronicle of the struggle between the Greek city states and the Persian empire? As we have seen, Ricoeur considers both to be rooted in narrativity. The major difference, for him, is simply that *poiēsis*, so to speak, carries its world within itself, and has various means—as in the storyteller's "once upon a time" and its many equivalents—of announcing its own independence of historical reality. History, on the other hand, opens itself to correction and invalidation. As Ricoeur once remarked, it would be pointless to set two novels or plays about the French Revolution beside each other and ask which, in a purely factual sense, was the more accurate. Yet this is something we do automatically with two *histories* of the French Revolution. That is why it is important to Ricoeur, as we shall see, that in history even invalidation is ultimately based on narrativity. One asserts a rival claim about historical truth, in his view, not only by producing new facts but by then invoking them to tell an alternative story about the past.

Chapter Five

POETICS OF HISTORY

RICOEUR'S TREATMENT OF HISTORICAL WRITING IN *TIME AND Narrative* involves a paradox. His ostensible subject is the problem of representing a past that is no longer there. Yet it will turn out that his aim has been, all along, to show that in a certain sense we already inhabit that past. Ricoeur's ultimate point will be that the temporality we inhabit as social beings—what he will call "narrated time" (*le temps raconté*) or the "third time" of narrativity—is a time of volition and preoccupation intelligible only in narrative terms. This will be, for him, both the time of ordinary existence and the ground of truth in historical narrative. It is a "third time" because it stands apart both from Aristotle's cosmic time or "time of the world" and Augustine's phenomenological "time of the soul," the only two concepts to have emerged from centuries of philosophical speculation. It is "narrated time" because, as a temporality fundamentally continuous with that of earlier generations who also understood themselves and their cultures in terms of stories, it underlies both the written and unwritten narratives of human existence.

Ricoeur's conception of narrated time is very close to Heidegger's time of *Sorge*. Dasein—Heidegger's term, we recall, for human consciousness as "thrown" into a world it did not make—is always "ahead of itself" in the sense that it understands itself in terms of its possibilities. The difference between you or me and a rock or a tree or a groundhog is that we may choose among various possibilities, deciding, say, either to study piano at a conservatory rather than going to medical school, or, less momentously, to go fishing this afternoon rather than to clean out the garage. This is why, for Heidegger, Dasein's mode of being in the world already implies the notions of a "future" and "having a project." The idea of *Sorge*—which includes, as we have seen, the more ordinary ideas of investment or concern or preoccupation—then arises from Dasein's sense of its own limits, or what Heidegger calls its "being toward death."

Limitation means significance: the value of what one chooses emerges from comparison with other, excluded choices. For Ricoeur, the single most important truth set forth in *Being and Time* is that we are born into a world made up of meaning or significance. This is the world of *Sorge*. Only if Dasein is care, says Heidegger, can it inhabit a significant world, and only if it inhabits a significant world can Dasein be care. This is the sort of pronouncement that has made European philosophy, to some Anglo-American ears, seem little more than a traffic in dubious profundities. But in fact there is a serious challenge here. What Heidegger is demanding at such moments is nothing less than a total inversion of the empiricist perspective often taken for granted in Anglo-American philosophy, for which the world starts out as a domain independent of human significance—the *res extensa* of Cartesian rationalism, say, or the whirl of subatomic particles that is the material reality of modern physics. In this view of the world, one picks out X or Y from a neutral field of meaningless objects and only then "adds" significance, as when the botanical entity I carry in my hand is somehow changed, in transit, into the rose I give my love.

Ricoeur, for reasons I discuss shortly, disagrees with Heidegger about the nature of historical time. The one point that will survive this disagreement, and that will then count as the major Heideggerian contribution to Ricoeur's own argument, is that the world is significant for us before it becomes objective. The baby picks out its mother or the ball dancing on a string above its crib as being more "meaningful" than the distant wall. The rose I carry to my love is first of all a flower and a token of my feeling, and only then, if at all, the object described by botanists in terms of genus and species. For Heidegger, it is through relentless abstraction away from a world full of meaning that an "objective" world of things-in-themselves—and, subsequently, of atoms and molecules, muons and pions—comes to be constituted. For Ricoeur, what matters is the reality that exists before such abstraction gets under way. Only when we have seen that the world in which consciousness moves and has its being is *already* meaningful or significant, he thinks, are we in a position to think clearly about time and history.

Heidegger's position is that ordinary time is false or inauthentic because it attempts to deny the finitude or being-toward-death in which *Sorge* originates. Ricoeur thinks this notion of inauthenticity misplaced. Even here, however, he wants to retain certain insights drawn from Heidegger's analysis. This is the case, for instance, with what Heidegger imagines as an original linking of care to cosmological time, the implications of which become apparent as soon as we think about an earlier epoch when daylight would have been purely a "time of preoccupation" for tasks impossible in darkness. With this linking, says Heidegger, begins a fall into the impersonality of ordinary time, with instruments—sundials, hourglasses, clocks—meant to provide a more "exact" way of dividing up the day into units with less and less relation to the sun as a bringer of light. This fall is complete when an "ordinary time" of hours, minutes, and seconds has become the dominant social reality. By the end, the sun itself will seem to move to the hands of the clock, as when we are told that sunrise tomorrow will occur at precisely 5:32 a.m.

Ricoeur's disagreement is about the implications of this notion of loss or estrangement. We pass to ordinary time, Heidegger argued, only through a series of "forgettings" that gradually loses touch with a world organized entirely in terms of concern—my total absorption in my task, say, when I am making something at my workbench, or trying to learn a difficult piece of music on the piano—and leads us, instead, to dwell in a separate or autonomous time. From this, the time of clocks and committees and appointments, follows a loss of authenticity and resoluteness in the face of being-toward-death. But the very notion of resoluteness, we have seen, amounts in Ricoeur's view to an ungrounded neostoicism having no essential relation to Heidegger's account of *Sorge*. Nor can it support the scaffolding of progressively false temporalities on which Heidegger bases his analysis. This is why we arrive at a truer perspective on historical time, argues Ricoeur, only when we have detached the idea of a time of *Sorge* from what Theodor Adorno unkindly called Heidegger's "jargon of authenticity."

In particular, Ricoeur wants to link the idea to what he calls the logic of the trace. Given a time of *Sorge*, what sense are we to make of a past inhabited by beings we feel to have been like ourselves? To what extent does a difference in culture or period make them beings different, perhaps unimaginably different, from us? Our time of dates and calendars assures us that their existence had a determinate relation to our own. The world history timeline on the schoolroom wall does demonstrate, after all, that the neolithic hunter-gatherers came before the Babylonians and Assyrians, and that European explorers set out for the New World some centuries after the collapse of the Roman empire. But if our question is whether their experience of the world was in some fundamental sense like our own, the schoolroom timeline does not seem to tell us anything very significant. Here, Heidegger's impatience with public or universal time can seem reasonable enough. The time of *Sorge*, however it might have been experienced by the neolithic hunter-gather or the ancient Roman, can hardly be measured in such terms.

How, then, are we to recover a past inhabited by beings who dwelt in a world of preoccupation or concern? This brings us to the problem of the trace, which for Ricoeur includes everything normally counted as historical evidence: a fossil footprint, a stone axe, the ruins of a temple, clay tablets covered with cuneiform writing, Greek manuscripts from a Renaissance library. Historical evidence always presupposes that the past has left a trace. But what, exactly, are we to mean by "trace"? As a first approximation, Ricoeur takes Emmanuel Lévinas's idea of the trace—it is, as he says, both a *thing* and a *sign*—as the disarrangement of some order that invites explanation in terms of an absent cause. So, for instance, the tracks of a wolf in the snow are a sign that "an animal has passed this way." A fossil trilobite survives as a sign of a teeming world of prehistoric life forms, a fossil footprint from the Olduvai Gorge as a sign of our earliest human ancestors. In the same way, the ruins of a Greek temple tell us, just as the tracks in the snow told us about the wolf, that "a people was once here."

To speak of the trace as a sign of the past, however, is to put something of a strain on our usual meaning of "sign," at least so far as that normally implies a desire to communicate. The problem is obvious. The wolf who left tracks in the snow had no intention of leaving a sign of his passing. The human ancestor who left a fossil footprint had no thought of leaving a trace for future generations, and probably no idea that he was doing so. The ruins of the Greek temple, it is true, may be taken as a sign in the more usual sense—the temple was meant, its builders might have explained, as an outward sign or symbol of their reverence for the gods—but not in the sense one has in mind when trying to date its inscriptions. The priestesses of Apollo could scarcely have been trying, after all, to communicate with twenty-first century archaeologists. Yet as soon as we ask about the intentions of the Greeks who built the temple—their beliefs, their rituals, their sense of the divine in everyday life—there is a break or rupture with the linear time of clocks and calendars and carbon-14 dating. We have entered, obviously, a time of care or preoccupation.

Heidegger's way of putting this was to say that the ruined temple is a trace of "a Dasein which has been there." But only a trace: since the world as it existed for that Dasein—or, say, for the remote human ancestor who left the fossil footprint—was not a mere physical setting but a way-of-being-in-the-world, it is in a certain important sense irrecoverable. It is, above all, not something that can be understood in terms of a uniform historical time. Ricoeur thinks, however, that this is not the point of historical dating. His reasons are, interestingly enough, profoundly Heideggerian. Consider: I find a stone axe. I see immediately that it belongs to a world different from my own, but also that it is not, like the stars or the mountains, part of the purely physical environment into which I was "thrown," the earth as it would have existed had no human beings appeared. So what, exactly, is the axe? It was, I see, a tool—part of Heidegger's world of human projects, the "ready to hand"—in a world that has now vanished. This alone is enough to tell me that its people were, like me, "thrown," had projects, and lived in a world of care.

The stone axe in itself tells us something about that world of projects that Heidegger called the *Umwelt* of Dasein. For a tool is never single, as Heidegger once remarked, but belongs to an entire web of significance. The pen with which I write this sentence assumes the existence of the paper on which I write, the table underneath, the book open on its stand before me, and, taken all together, the project on which I am now intent. In the same way, the stone axe implies the flint spearheads and arrowheads, the scrapers, the awls, the striking flints, the bone needles, and other tools that archaeologists have recovered from neolithic sites. Ricoeur's point about these would be that they tell a story, to those who have ears to hear, about a people who hunted, cooked their food over fires, scraped and cured the skins of animals, sewed these for use as clothing, lived together in a world of cooperative labor, had means of protecting themselves against predators, and possessed not only tools but, crucially for their connection to the world inhabited by us as their descendants, tools for making tools.

Heidegger was right to think that none of this is made comprehensible by a grand scheme of uniform historical time. What he failed to see, in Ricoeur's view, is that such time plays very little part in how we ordinarily make sense of the human past. We do not look at traces of a "Dasein that has been there" as inert evidence. We try, instead, to imagine the world of the maker of the stone axe as it existed for its inhabitants. At an intuitive level—a level so deep that it does not strike us as a conscious choice or "method"—we imagine it as a world of volition and action, of choices, motives, resentments, attachments, and the like. The people of the stone axe, we infer, hunted, stored food against the dearth of winter, had rituals for burying their dead. Ricoeur's point is that we tell ourselves "little stories" about this or that portion of the past—about *this* stone axe, *this* clay tablet—while at the same time understanding them as episodes in a human story that began with the emergence of Dasein and continues to the present moment.

Human time, in short, is always narrated time. We cannot connect ourselves to traces of the past without filling in the intervening time with the outlines of a story about humanity. The timeline that hangs on the schoolroom wall thus has less to do with Heidegger's universal time, Ricoeur would claim, than with a preliminary ordering of events that can only be understood in terms of narrative causality. To understand why Caesar's legions felt a personal loyalty to him, it will be necessary to establish that his campaign in Gaul took place before, and not after, his crossing of the Rubicon. To understand why Cro-Magnon man came gradually to displace the Neanderthals who had previously been successful in the same physical environment, it will be necessary to undertake exact dating of burial sites, tools, fossil remains, and other traces of both populations. But this is to put such techniques as carbon-14 dating at the service not of some uniform historical time but of a collective narrative, the recovery of the human past, one might say, as a Heideggerian project itself carried out in a time of preoccupation and concern.

Heidegger described the falsity of ordinary time as an endless succession of uniform "nows," none distinguishable from any other. His term for this mode of temporality was, in fact, *Jetzt-Zeit*, or "now-time." But for Ricoeur, *now* will always be instead a positive term referring to a time of mind or consciousness as it is linked to a repetition or regularity occurring independent of itself. We could imagine, we said earlier, an eternal pendulum that had been in motion since the beginning of the universe. Ricoeur's point is that this would not *in itself* measure time. Only the connection of a "now" of lived time to one of its movements could make it serve as a clock. Such connections do mark, as Heidegger saw, the origin of calendrical time, but Ricoeur's concern is only incidentally with origins. The more important point will be that the regularities associated with Aristotle's "time of the world"—the changing intervals of daylight and darkness, the phases of the moon, the wheeling of the constellations through the sky—can help determine, but cannot enumerate, the periods of calendrical time.

For Ricoeur, one important sign that calendrical systems involve an irreducible narrativity is that all societies have some version of what Émile Benveniste calls chronicle time, in which an originary event—the birth of Jesus or the Buddha, the Hegira, the *ab urbe condita* of the Romans—marks a point from which everything else can be measured. This is, for him, the counterpart at the collective or communal level of imposing a "now" of lived experience on the merely mechanical movements of the pendulum. Part of Ricoeur's point will thus be that in a world of purely physical time, the notion of an event that breaks with past events or inaugurates a new era—in *this* year Christ was crucified in Jerusalem, in *this* year Luther posted his Ninety-five Theses, in *this* year Lincoln issued the Emancipation Proclamation—would not be intelligible. But Ricoeur also wants us to see that the very notion of an originary event defines historical time as a "third time," the cultural medium within which individuals and societies live out their temporal existence.

How, then, do cultures sustain the narratives set in motion by an originary event? The answer, for Ricoeur, lies in a human generation conceived as what Alfred Schutz called a community in time, or what might equally be called a community formed *by* time. Ricoeur's own account is based on what Karl Mannheim in *Ideology and Utopia* called the "we relation" of contemporaries within a culture. The sense of one's own generation, Mannheim said, derives from experiences that leave the impress of a shared destiny—going through the Great Depression, remembering the Normandy landings, recalling the March on Washington—far stronger than the more contingent bonds that make one, say, a weekend golfer or a midwestern American. This in turn makes possible a connectedness between generations. The story told by a grandfather to his grandson is filled with people unknown to the child, but the we-relation with the grandfather then implies a we-relation between the old man and *his* grandfather. If I tell my grandchild a tale my grandfather told me, Ricoeur remarks, I am not only handing down a community in time but creating the time in which such a community exists.

A world crowded with meanings, Heidegger said, gives rise to linguistic distinctions: "to significations, words accrue." Ricoeur's point about narrativity as a human universal might be put in similar terms: to significant human actions, stories accrue. Within any human society, even at the most ordinary level of daily life, stories already serve to make intelligible a heterogeneous mix of motives, actions, and circumstances ungraspable in any other terms. At the collective level, narrative serves the same purpose in relation to a sense of shared destiny, placing nations or civilizations within what Ricoeur calls the "third time" of narrativity. This is why, in his view—what might be called Ricoeur's version of Dilthey's *Verstehen* principle—any meaningful account of the human past must itself operate in terms of narrative causality. As a contemporary historian, I may not think about my new history of Rome as a story, but it must nonetheless try to understand how and why the Romans understood their own origins through a story about twins suckled by a wolf.

How does narrative causality come to serve as historical explanation? For some philosophers of history, the answer has seemed to lie in the relation between an event and its consequences. Ricoeur considers, for instance, Arthur Danto's notion of the "narrative sentence" as the basic unit of historical writing. Through it, Danto means to challenge the naive idea of history as a true account of events in the past just as they happened. Imagine, says Danto in his *Analytic Philosophy of History*, an Ideal Chronicler, a superhuman intelligence or, as we might now be more disposed to say, a computer-satellite-video array, able to record all events in a given time period at the moment they occur. The point, when we pause to think about it, is obvious. The Chronicler would not be operating as a historian. The meaning of an event lies in its consequences, and this by definition is something the Chronicler cannot know. The Chronicler's record would be something like the jagged scrawl of an electrocardiogram before it has been interpreted by a physician. For the historian, Danto argues, interpretation will always take the form of a story about the past.

To bring out what he takes to be the narrative structure of historical explanation, Danto analyzes such sentences as "In 1717, the author of *Rameau's Nephew* was born." If we adopt a simple notation, this brings to light a structure of $E_1 \rightarrow E_2 \leftarrow T$, where the point is to put one event (E_1)—a baby is born—in relation to another (E_2)—Diderot's composition of *Rameau's Nephew*—while both are in the past in relation to T, the time of utterance. Danto's way of putting this is to say that the historian describes both the original event and its consequence in *their* past. As Ricoeur points out, however, this leaves an unresolved problem. Danto's analysis *already* assumes an unexamined notion of narrative causality, which here operates as a rule of relevance guiding the selection of events. Simply asserting a relation between any two temporally separate events—Hitler's widely publicized vegetarianism in the early 1930s, say, and the subsequent collapse of the Chicago futures market in pork bellies—cannot establish a *connection*. The missing element in Danto's analysis, says Ricoeur, is plot.

The writer who comes closest to grasping this point, Ricoeur thinks, is W. B. Gallie, who argues that history always originates in or proceeds from an actual or implied narrative—for instance, the story of

Romulus and Remus and all that follows in the early books of Livy, as a key to the way the Romans understood themselves—and then remains in the service of the narrative form. This double requirement establishes what Gallie, in his *Philosophy and the Historical Understanding*, calls the "followability" of any historical account, which Ricoeur sees as corresponding to Aristotle's *telos* of emplotment. For Gallie, as for Ricoeur, the notion of "story" involves an abstract structure common to history and fiction. It consists, says Gallie, of (1) a series of actions or experiences done or undergone by real or imaginary people, while (2) these people are portrayed either in situations that change or as reacting to such change, whereupon (3) these changes reveal unexpected aspects of the situation or people involved, such that (4) a new predicament calling for thought or action is engendered. This sequence then posits a teleological development that operates in terms of narrative causality. "Ideally," says Gallie, "a story should be self-explanatory."[1]

In Aristotle's account of *mythos*, a story is self-explanatory in the sense that we intuitively grasp the "internal" relation between events. Oedipus puts out his eyes, we understand, because looking any longer on a world where he has committed parricide and incest has become intolerable to him. But in what sense can a history, even when it comes to us in narrative form, be self-explanatory in this way? Ricoeur's answer is that narrative causality is always rooted in the semantics of action, and that historical events are intelligible only insofar as they are grounded in the actions of individual agents. "Events," he says at one point, "are what active agents make happen," which is why "events share in the contingency proper to action."[2] If I act in such-and-such a way, my action demands interpretation because I might have chosen to act otherwise. If you tell yourself a story to explain my action—"the real reason he got up to get a drink of water is that he wanted to cover up his embarrassment"—then events rooted in that action will belong to the same story.

In historical narrative, however, we find ourselves dealing more or less constantly with larger-scale events—for example, "Japan bombed Pearl Harbor"—that do not seem to answer in any direct way to this same semantics of action. Here we discover why Ricoeur wants to claim that what he calls first-order entities—nations, peoples, classes, civilizations—actually do operate as characters in history. The reason is that individuals are related to such entities, and to each other within them, through what he calls an experience of participatory belonging. This is a much stronger claim than that, being a citizen of the United States, I in some unspecified sense feel myself to be American. It is the claim that, coming naked into the world, I absorbed my American identity just as I absorbed English as my native language: my attitudes, my values, my customs, my sense of my own family and group within the larger social whole, and a great deal more derive from my perception of "America" as a society or community that in a certain sense exists independent of me.

This is why Ricoeur wants to insist that first-order entities may never be treated—this was Dray's mistake—as simply the sum total of the individuals who make them up. I may disagree with much that is done in the name of America—though I might also think of this disagreement as being characteristically American—and I may feel closer or less close to this or that group within the social whole. But all this will be grounded in my sense that "America" is a collective character in a historical story, and—just as important—that those in other national communities are viewing themselves in the same way. When the news about Pearl Harbor came over a million radios, no one in Japan or America would have taken it as an action by an unattached group of pilots. Indeed, the pilots themselves understood that it was "Japan," and not they, that was bombing Pearl Harbor. In the immediate aftermath, it was similarly understood that it was the United States, and not this or that congressman or senator, that was declaring war on Japan.

The point about such episodes is not that narratives may be constructed about them, but that they are grasped from the first instant in narrative terms. Pearl Harbor, whatever else it may have come to signify, could in its own moment only be understood as the opening scene in a momentous historical drama. This is the basis of Ricoeur's claim that, in all such cases, a *plot* is assigning collective entities like "Japan" and "America" roles as characters in a story. For "character," Ricoeur reminds us—drawing on Greimas's theory of the "actant"—describes not a person but a *function*: whatever is able to fill the place allotted to X in the formula "X does R." Whether we are speaking about persons or nations will then depend entirely on the semantic level. "Japan ate a grape" is clearly nonsense, as is "Peter bombed Pearl Harbor." But once the semantic level is established, "Japan bombed Pearl Harbor" belongs as legitimately to narrative discourse as "Peter ate a grape."

For Ricoeur, the great virtue of Gallie's theory is that it is able to assign entities such as "Germany" or "the Persian empire" a meaningful role in historical narrative in a way corresponding to their actual role in historical experience. This is what sustains an intelligible notion of plot—what Ricoeur calls a "quasi-plot"—at the level of collective motive and action. Thus, statements made at this higher level—"Germany felt humiliated by the provisions of the Versailles Treaty," "Germany rejoiced at the reoccupation of the Rhineland as a vindication of national honor"—remain entirely meaningful even when they include any number of individual exceptions. There were, as we know, Germans who did not feel the provisions of the Versailles Treaty to be wholly unjust. There were many who did not rejoice at the reoccupation of the Rhineland. But these individuals would not have dissented from the proposition that "Germany" felt humiliated, or that "Germany" rejoiced. Ricoeur's "quasi-plot" is in this sense simply plot as it plays a dominant role in collective experience.

The weakness of Gallie's theory, on the other hand, is that it provides no way of accounting for the "grasping together" of heterogeneous elements within an event, or the "internal" relation of events within the story as a whole, which is the essence of narrative causality. This is Louis O. Mink's objection to Gallie. Gallie's "series of events" seems to constitute a narrative, Mink argues, only because we intuitively understand the events as being driven forward toward a predetermined conclusion. But as Gallie himself describes his conception of "story," its events might simply be a self-generating series that leads nowhere in particular, or that simply degenerates into randomness. What Gallie is missing, says Mink, is what we earlier heard Boethius call the *totum simul* perspective—that is, events viewed as a single or simultaneous whole, as God would view them from outside time. In historical narrative, Mink points out, this is precisely the relation of the historian to the events being related.

Mink's objection has obvious implications for any theory of narrative history. Without a narrative *telos*—that forward-straining tension that links each event to the next within the plot—there can be no story. But unless events are moving toward an outcome already implicit in their development, there can be no *telos*. This is the problem Mink wants to solve simply by emphasizing that in historical narrative the outcome is by definition known to the historian: "history is not the writing, but the rewriting of stories." What underwrites the *telos* of historical plot, by the same token, is that events lead *necessarily* to this conclusion: "the story that began with Hitler's reoccupation of the Rhineland would end, less than ten years later, with his suicide in a Berlin bunker, followed by Germany's surrender to the Allies." It is not that the story could not have turned out otherwise—the fate of nations hung in the balance a hundred times during these years—but that they did not. "There are," as Mink puts it, "no contingencies going backwards."[3]

Ricoeur's own theory of historical narrative combines what he takes to be the valid elements of Mink's and Gallie's positions. Thus, Mink's notion of a *totum simul* perspective will always remain pertinent, for instance, because it alone permits the historian to link conscious intentions and unintended consequences, as when the assassination of the Archduke Franz Ferdinand set in motion the events that would lead to the carnage of World War I. Yet there always hovers over such narration, Ricoeur points out, the danger of what Raymond Aron called "the retrospective illusion of fatality." The historian may forget that this was, to the people who lived it, not an inevitable sequence of doomlike developments but an anxious, often terrifying, series of contingencies whose end no human eye could see. The particular virtue of Gallie's more open-ended position is that it insists on preserving what Ricoeur once calls the "space of contingency," in which history is actually made and experienced, and in which human volition never ceases to operate as a force in determining the outcome.

Historical events, R. G. Collingwood famously said, have an inside and an outside. He meant, as we saw in chapter 4, an inside so far as they involve human motive and purpose, an outside so far as they take place in or are determined by external circumstances. For Ricoeur, both inside and outside represent aspects of a reality grasped primarily in narrative terms. This is the key to his poetics of history. We understand historical events, in his view, only as they are rooted in the more general semantics of action that underlies the spontaneous and unremarked narrativity of everyday life. So understood, events become occurrences within a common or collective narrative time. The same semantics of action explains,

he thinks, why human beings in any age or society are disposed to experience larger-scale events—wars, invasions, natural cataclysms—in
terms of something that seems to be, even before its outcome can possibly be known, a "plot of history." All this is what Ricoeur has in mind
in insisting that "historical events do not differ radically from the events
framed by a plot" ("événements encadrés par une intrigue").[4]

In Ricoeur's own French intellectual tradition, the greatest challenge to an idea of history rooted in the semantics of individual action came from the *Annales* school founded by Marc Bloch and Lucien
Febvre in the 1920s, and given monumental status in Fernand Braudel's
La Méditerranée et le monde Méditerranéan dans l'époch de Philippe II
in 1949. For on the *Annales* view of history, individuals and their actions dwindle into virtual nothingness in relation to the *longue durée*,
or the centuries-long processes of geophysical, institutional, and economic change and the slow, almost imperceptible shifting of civilizations, within which particular societies live out their short lives. This
is the history that Foucault is speaking about at the beginning of *The
Archaelogy of Knowledge*: "Beneath the rapidly changing history of gov-
ernments, wars, and famines, there emerge other, apparently unmoving
histories: the history of sea routes, the history of corn or of gold-mining,
the history of drought and of irrigation, the history of crop rotation, the
history of the balance achieved by the human species between hunger
and abundance."[5]

In theory, Braudel's *La Méditerranée* ought to have banished anything recognizable as plot. For "plot" as a concept seems to belong to the
narrative form that the *Annales* historians dismissed as *l'histoire événementielle*: kings, diplomats, battles, and "events" as something always
taking place, as Lucien Febvre once said, in the brief span of individual
lives. As an alternative, Braudel gives us three distinct time spans. The
first, which he calls *l'histoire quasi immobile*, is the world of the Mediterranean before human settlement, a landscape of mountains and rivers
and coastal lands subject only to the imperceptible forces of geological
change. The second is the *longue durée* proper, the time of what Braudel
calls "conjunctures": trade patterns, changes in modes of transportation,
the emergence of monetary systems, and so forth. Finally, at the top-
most level, comes the clash of Christian and Islamic civilization with
the rivalry of Spain and Turkey in the time of Philip II, after which, says

Braudel, Spain would turn its back on Europe and look to a new world of silver and conquest in America.

Yet Ricoeur, in an analysis as brilliant in its own way as Braudel's great work, sees here both a story and a plot. For even at the "time-less" level of Braudel's empty landscape, it is the arrival of human be-ings that gives meaning or significance to its features, as the mountains become the refuge of "free" men, the fertile coastlines are settled by colonists, and trade among peoples makes the sea itself into a great net-work of intercommunication. At the second level, trading centers such as Genoa, Venice, and Florence begin to give a recognizable shape to a world in which commerce, competition, and the growth of states are altering the lives of each new generation. Here, even Braudel himself acknowledges that something very like emplotment is at work. The his-tory of the Mediterranean in the sixteenth century, he says, is the story of two leviathans—he means Christian Europe, represented by Spain, and the Islamic East, represented by Ottoman Turkey—taking up their positions. The clash then comes, at the level of events, when the forces of Philip and Selim II face each other in the battle of Lepanto.

The actual importance of the battle of Lepanto was absurdly over-estimated by both contemporary witnesses and its protagonists. As Ricoeur notes, Voltaire was already mocking its claims to historical sig-nificance in the eighteenth century. It may be taken to represent what the *Annales* historians saw as the inevitable superficiality of *l'histoire événementielle*, or history as viewed through the eyes of rulers, generals, admirals, diplomats, and those who travel in their train. But for Ricoeur, the battle and its aftermath play very little part in the grand narrative sweep of *La Méditerranée*, in which the Mediterranean world must be understood as the collective hero in a story about world history, and in which the vast shift that takes place when Spain turns away from the Old World and toward the New World and its silver, entering into a transatlantic rivalry with the English and the Dutch, marks the banish-ment or exile of the hero. The plot of Braudel's story, says Ricoeur, is the decline of the Mediterranean as a historical zone; its denouement is the exit of the Mediterranean from the spotlight of world history.

Ricoeur's analysis of *La Méditerranée* is an exemplary demonstra-tion of a key concept in his larger theory of mimesis. This concept is what we might call double temporality, or the idea that a story moves forward for those within its horizon of events but backward from the *totum simul* perspective of a narrator who knows its outcome and has drawn his or her conclusions about its meaning. In his discussion of *La Méditerranée*, Ricoeur once says that to be truly understood, narrative must read simultaneously forward and backward ("d'avant en arrière et d'arrière en avant"). Ricoeur's "backwards" reading of *La Méditerranée* starts from the death of Philip II and moves back into the increasingly depopulated spaces of the Mediterranean lands, ending in a world of mountains and rivers and coastal plains largely empty of any human presence. What he shows is that the people of Braudel's story, during their forward movement, have only incidentally been migrating from one island or isthmus or peninsula to another. They have been moving, all unawares, into nothing other than narrated time.

Chapter Six

POETICS OF FICTION

AMONG THE EARLY READERS OF THOMAS CARLYLE'S *THE FRENCH Revolution* was the young Charles Dickens, who read Carlyle's sweeping historical narrative numerous times between its appearance in 1839 and the moment he sat down to write *A Tale of Two Cities* nearly twenty years later. To Victorian readers, used to thinking of historical writing as a literary art, the strong resemblance between the two works would have seemed entirely unremarkable. Each had a compelling narrative drive, moving irresistibly forward a conclusion tinged with something very like tragic inevitability. Both were based on research and documentation, as well as the living memories of those who had survived to hand down their personal stories. The voices of their narrators—the one unforgettably "Carlylean," the other just as unmistakably "Dickensian"—would have been instantly recognizable to anyone familiar with contemporary literary culture. Yet for Victorian readers, as for us now, it was also clear that one could only be called a work of history, the other a work of fiction.

How, then, to account for the distinction? For Ricoeur, the key is that Carlyle's story takes place in historical time, a unified spatiotemporal framework within which any location or event may be precisely located in relation to any other. Dickens's story, on the other hand, takes place in what we have heard Ricoeur call fictive time, the imaginary past formally declared by the narrator's opening sentence, "It was the best of times, it was the worst of times," and established within a few more sentences as the reality in which characters like Charles Darnay and Sydney Carton, Miss Pross and Madame Defarge, will have their being. Both historical time and fictive time are, in Ricoeur's view, versions of that "third time" of narrative in which a consciousness otherwise marooned in a blind material universe discovers a mirror of its own world of human concerns. History, by virtue of its claims to objectivity and empirical confirmation, nonetheless remains tied to Aristotle's "time of the world," to clocks and calendrical systems as these relate to the movement of the sun and planets and constellations.

Fictive time, on the other hand, is closer to Augustine's "time of the soul," which operates independent of clock time, as when the same hour that seems interminable to me, bored while waiting for an appointment, passes in a flash for you, intensely absorbed in playing chess or watching a film. It is older than historical time—there has been no human community, we recall Barthes saying, without narrative—and stretches back, as the time internal to epic and saga and tales told round the fire, into a prehistory whose outlines we glimpse only dimly. It testifies, preeminently, to a need of story for its own sake, to the human need to impose a narrative order on the buzz and confusion of the world. "Fictions are not simply arbitrary," Ricoeur once says—he is discussing, at this point, Frank Kermode's *The Sense of Ending*—"inasmuch as they respond to a need over which we are not the masters, the need to impress the stamp of order upon the chaos of existence [le besoin d'imprimer le sceau de l'ordre sur le chaos], of sense upon nonsense, of concordance upon discordance."[1]

For Ricoeur, Harald Weinrich's analysis of the "narrative preterite" convincingly demonstrates the means through which fictional narrative emancipates itself from historical time: the "once upon a time" of fairy tales or *Märchen*, the invocations of the heavenly Muse in epic, or the past tense of the European novel. Nonetheless, fictional narrative seems to retain a lingering attachment to the "real," taking over into its imaginary world actual buildings, real streets, historical personages and datable events, landscapes that one might get up and actually walk through after putting down the novel in which they were described. So, for instance, Carlyle writes about the storming of the Bastille in *The French Revolution* as an epochal event in historical time, taking place on July 14,

1789. On what grounds, then, are we to say that Dickens, recounting the same event in *A Tale of Two Cities*, is describing actions taking place in an imaginary time? Is the date not the same? Is not the Bastille, at least, the actual prison, identical in both accounts? Here is Dickens:

> Cannon, muskets, fire and smoke; but, still the deep ditch, the single drawbridge, the massive stone walls, and the eight great towers. Slight displacements of the raging sea, made by the falling wounded. Flashing weapons, blazing torches, smoking wagon-loads of wet straw, hard work at neighbouring barricades in all directions, shrieks, volleys, execrations, bravery without stint, boom, smash and rattle, and the furious sounding of the living sea; but, still the deep ditch, and the single drawbridge, and the massive stone walls, and the eight great towers, and still Defarge of the wine-shop at his gun, grown doubly hot by the service of four fierce hours.[2]

Ricoeur's answer is that Dickens's eight-towered prison belongs solely to an imaginary setting existing outside historical time. The difference between historical and fictional narrative becomes intelligible, he argues, once we have seen its resemblance to what analytic philosophy calls the use-mention distinction. If, for instance, I say "Please shut the door behind you," I am *using* the word "door" to refer to something independent of my utterance. If, on the other hand, I say "The word 'door' has four letters," I am *mentioning* the same word to make a remark about English orthography. For Ricoeur, the crucial point is that in the first case I am, so to speak, asking you to look "through" the word *door* to an external reality. In the second, I am asking you to look "at" *door* as something internal to my utterance. In the same way, one looks "through" Carlyle's description to an external reality that invites comparison with other historical accounts. But Dickens's Bastille is simply mentioned as one feature of a setting already established, on quite separate grounds, as belonging to an imagined world.

Fictive time thus becomes the basis of Ricoeur's insistence on literary autonomy, or the principle that every fictional work is a self-contained world with its own laws and its own logic, separate from external systems of value or belief. This is the basis on which he undertakes a radical reconsideration of the *totum simul* perspective, which now becomes not simply the position of the narrator—that fixed point toward which the *telos* of the story is steadily tending, occupied by a narrator who already knows the outcome—but the more abstract position from which the story may be grasped as a total structure of meaning or significance. Thus considered, the *totum simul* becomes a position that may or may not coincide with the narrator's point of view, but that nonetheless exists within every narrative structure as an ideal possibility. To see how the point bears on the more fundamental problem of fictive time, let us briefly consider Ricoeur's discussion of temporal conscious and narrative structure in three novels: Virginia Woolf's *Mrs Dalloway*, Thomas Mann's *The Magic Mountain*, and Proust's *Remembrance of Things Past*.[3]

Each of these three novels is what the narrator of *The Magic Mountain* calls a *Zeitroman*, or "time-novel." Ricoeur refers to them as "tales about time" ("fables sur le temps"), meaning that their subject is temporality in the same sense that, say, parliamentary politics is the subject of Trollope's Palliser novels. His analysis in each case explores what we have called the double temporality of narrative structure: a *telos* that carries characters forward in a state of imperfect knowledge about the consequences of their actions, with a narrator who, gazing backward on events from a fixed or *totum simul* perspective, has arrived at certain conclusions about their meaning or significance. What gives each its status as a tale about time is that its moment of *anagnorisis* or recognition—that climactic instant at which *telos* and *totum simul* converge—permits readers fully to grasp their own immersion in the story as having been an interlude or parenthesis within the mortal time of their own existence. This experience, normally taken for granted when reading, is what Ricoeur will call the fictive experience of time ("l'expérience temporelle fictive").

In *Mrs Dalloway*, the focus is on two major characters for whom ordinary existence has become a thin crust through which one might at any instant fall into an abyss of pure despair. One of the two, Septimus Harding, a young veteran of the Great War, is falling into that abyss during the time of the story, a day in June 1923. He has begun to hear the voices of dead comrades and to see diabolic faces—"faces laughing at him, calling him horrible disgusting names"—jeering from depths below. He will, later this day, commit suicide by jumping from a high window. The other character, Clarissa Dalloway, is the wife of a government minister, a "perfect hostess," as an old lover once mockingly tells her, and someone for whom, as for Septimus, a terrible conviction that the universe is utterly meaningless haunts every waking thought. "She always had the feeling," the narrator tells us, "that it was very, very dangerous to live even one day." The story begins with Clarissa's preparations for a grand party she is to give that night. It ends that evening, when the last guests are preparing to depart.

The story is set in central London. During the course of the day, external time is marked by Big Ben—"There! Out it boomed. First a warning, musical; then the hour, irrevocable. The leaden circles dissolved in the air"—and reported by the narrator in terms that emphasize its connection to an official time of meetings and government committees, a world of busy self-importance acting out an empty charade of meaning or purpose. Yet the custodian of this time, remarkably enough, is the narrator, who is the only one conscious of Big Ben's striking as it is heard at various intervals and in different locations, as she also is the only one conscious of the totality of the physical setting in which events take place. In a world of isolated souls, the unity of a single narrative consciousness thus holds together a myriad of comings and goings, permitting us to understand, for instance, that Septimus and Clarissa, though wholly unknown to each other, are prey to a nearly identical sense of tragic futility. The story will reach its climax when the narrator, renouncing her role as outward observer, joins Clarissa Dalloway in the world of inner time.

That moment arrives when Sir William Bradshaw, a psychiatrist who, to Clarissa, is the living embodiment of an oppressive social conformity—"they make life intolerable, men like that"—mentions the suicide of Septimus. ("Oh! thought Clarissa, in the middle of my party, here's death.") Yet not death merely, but a self-chosen exit from despair, which leads Clarissa to embrace Septimus's choice as, in a sense, her own. As she does so, the narrator's own voice becomes, as Ricoeur says, inseparable from the other two ("le narrateur réunit en une seule voix narrative la sienne, celle de Septimus, et celle de Clarissa"): "Death was defiance. Death was an attempt to communicate . . . closeness drew apart; rapture faded; one was alone. There was an embrace in death." It is an extraordinary moment of *anagnorisis*, in which, as the narrator joins her thoughts to Clarissa's, "official" time is suddenly negated and the novel ends in a time of the soul: "the young man who had killed himself. She felt glad that he had done it; thrown it away while they went on living. The clock was striking. The leaden circles dissolved in the air."

The plot of Thomas Mann's *The Magic Mountain* is well known. Hans Castorp, a young engineer from Hamburg, comes to visit his cousin at the Berghof, a tuberculosis sanitorium high in the pure mountain air that was formerly thought to offer a chance of cure for those with the disease. While there, he is himself diagnosed with tuberculosis. The rest of the novel is the story of his experiences during seven years as a patient—his infatuation with Madame Chauchat, a fellow patient, his long conversations with Settembrini, an Italian writer, and with Naphta, a radical critic of bourgeois ideology, and his own slow adjustment to clinical life—but also, in what Ricoeur sees partly as a *Bildungsroman* and partly as a parody of the *Bildungsroman* form, the revelations that come to Castorp while, in the relentless sameness of life in the sanatorium, time disappears in favor of a perpetual or timeless duration. The great division in the novel is between "those down below"—the busy world of clocks and schedules—and "those up here," where the sick and dying seem to themselves frozen in time and space.

Ricoeur's analysis of *The Magic Mountain* is detailed and intricate, but its essential point is readily enough grasped. It is that the novel, unexpectedly reversing the normal relation between a forward-straining *telos* of plot and the *totum simul* perspective of the voice telling the story, is ultimately not about Castorp but about its own narrator. Or better, perhaps, about Thomas Mann, so long as we take the name to refer to "the narrative voice that, from place to place, calls upon the reader and expounds on his hero": the busy, intrusive, ironic consciousness of a storyteller who very often seems less interested in Castorp than in his own thoughts about the various alterations of consciousness the young engineer experiences during his stay at the Berghof.[4] In the main, as Ricoeur observes, these thoughts concern the way our ordinary sense of time is bound up with a consciousness of life (*Lebensgefühl*) so inseparable from routine activity that any protracted interruption lays bare a monotony or vacuity that was, all along, the unsuspected ground of our existence.

The Magic Mountain thus becomes, for Ricoeur, a series of false epiphanies, as its young protagonist works his way through to an ironic detachment—Mann calls this *Gedankenschärfe*, which Ricoeur terms *lucidité* or clarity of perception—that its narrator has known since the opening pages. The epiphanies are associated with *Ewigskeitsüppe*—"eternity soup," or the clinical time in which exactly the same broth is brought to patients at the exactly the same hour each day; with *Walpurgisnacht*, the ghastly and dreamlike carnival sequence during which the hero imagines mystical union with Madame Chauchat; and with *Schnee*, in which all awaken to find the landscape covered with snow, an unrelieved whiteness that looks like a vision of eternity. Then history intervenes. The Great War, or what the narrator calls "that universal feast of death," breaks out. Hans Castorp is called to arms, comes down off the mountain, and "in the tumult, in the rain, in the dusk, vanishes out of our sight." At the end, we are left alone with the narrator, but also with a clarity of perception denied to Castorp himself, made possible through the fictive experience of time.

In Proust's *Remembrance of Things Past*, Ricoeur thinks, we understand the problem of time only if we stay aware of the need to keep separate the voices of the hero—a somewhat bumptious bourgeois who, through a thousand pages, drags his boredom, as Ricoeur once says, from one silly salon to another ("d'un salon inept à l'autre")—and the narrator, whose great revelation about the relation of art to eternity comes only at the climax of the story, and who throughout is always ahead of the hero's progress because he is, as Ricoeur also says, surveying it from above ("est en avance sur la progression du héros parce qu'il la survole").[5] This is not to say that the narrator's voice is absent in the earlier portions of the story—it is there, though scarcely present as anything more than a murmur or an undertone—but only to say that the narrator is consciously recreating the voice of an earlier self, one that is lost, wandering, and yet moving steadily toward a final disillusionment that then, as though in a sudden mystical vision, gives way to his conversion to a vocation as an artist.

Ricoeur's argument is that *Remembrance* has been too narrowly understood as a story about the power of involuntary memory—not simply the famous madeleine episode, after which, as he says, Combray springs out of a cup of tea, but the various other "happy moments" ("moments bienheureux") that punctuate the narrative until the final scene of the great visitation in the Guermantes' library. Yet it is not strange that the story has been read this way, Ricoeur thinks, for an essential part of its ultimate meaning is that the hero himself misunderstands these same moments. They have for him no meaning beyond themselves, invariably dropping back, after their brief appearance, into the depths of forgotten experience. The protagonist who reappears in Paris at the very end of the story, Ricoeur reminds us, having been away for protracted stays at two different sanatoriums in hopes of curing the disease that is slowly wasting him away, is suffering grievously from an inward "absence of emotion." He is unhappily convinced of "the falsehood of literature," in whose redemptive power he had once put his faith, and utterly demoralized by "the non-existence of the ideal in which I had believed."[6]

The Marcel of the great revelation in the Guermantes' library, on the other hand, is someone who becomes suddenly aware that literature, which for him has so far been a mode of merely aesthetic experience, is, for the artist who creates it and the reader to whom it holds out the possibility of inward change, nothing other than a mode of self-revelation: "Real life, life at last laid bare and illuminated—the only life in consequence which can be said to be really lived—is literature, and life thus defined is in a sense all the time immanent in ordinary men no less than in the artist. But most men do not see it because they do not seek to shed light upon it."[7] The moment at which the narrator makes this discovery—and it is important to Ricoeur's argument that we are only now, at the very end of this vast and sprawling work, hearing the narrator's voice as such for the first time—occurs as what seems to him to have been a suspension of time ("l'être extra-temporel"). This is the position from which the true artist gazes through ordinary existence to realities that are outside time.

The promise of the madeleine is thus redeemed through a vision of art that has permitted us to glimpse a reality otherwise hidden from view. The truth of art is a truth of recognition, in the same sense as, staring unseeingly at a crowd, we suddenly recognize the face of a friend: the discovery of what, although we did not yet realize it, we already knew. Yet this is, after all, a reality knowable only within mortal existence. For Ricoeur, this is the point of the Guermantes' last dinner party, a *danse macabre* in which Marcel is initially unable to recognize the aged men and women who are the other guests. Among these aging puppets, marionettes of time whose younger selves he knew intimately, Marcel realizes that he is present at a recognition scene. It was necessary, he says, "to study them at the same time with one's eyes and one's memory," "to read what was written on several planes at once, planes that lay behind the visible aspect of the puppets and gave them depth."[8] The scene thus stands as Proust's parting admonition to the reader: the story that has carried you away must end, like all stories, by restoring you to the world of mortal time.

In these three novels, the *totum simul* perspective is more or less identical with that of the narrator. Yet this leaves open an important question about narrative structure. What are we to make of the narrator's role when the two do not coincide? In Ricoeur's view, understanding the meaning or significance of narrative begins in understanding two limitations of this role. The first is that the narrator is always, like his or her audience, a mere observer of events, able to react or respond to what is going on but powerless to intervene—as when the narrator of *Tom Jones* jokingly tells us, for instance, that he has begun to fall in love with his heroine. This is, for Ricoeur, the most important aspect of what Weinrich calls the narrative past tense. For now what it makes plain is not simply that the story must always take place in the past of the narrative voice, but that temporal discontinuity becomes ontological discontinuity. The narrator of *Pride and Prejudice* can no more interfere in the world of Elizabeth and Darcy than you and I can intervene in some past event in our own lives. Ricoeur cites Benveniste, who remarks that the past tense in narrative discourse designates not only "events that took place at a certain moment in time," but that are understood to have done so "without any intervention of the speaker."[9]

The second limitation has to do with the narrator's relation to characters in the story as what Ricoeur, drawing on the work of Käte Hamburger, Dorrit Cohn, and other narratologists, calls "centers of fictive consciousness" ("centres de conscience fictifs").[10] This, too, involves the notion of ontological discontinuity. When a character in a novel speaks, not only are we hearing the voice of a volitional being—that is, someone with independent motives, feelings, purposes, goals, and the ability to decide or choose among them—but the narrator's discourse, and the separate reality to which it belongs, are for that moment suspended. As the narrator has no power to intervene in events, in short, he or she is without power to impinge in any way on the consciousness of characters in the story. Ricoeur's way of putting this is to say that narrative voice in fiction is always *"the discourse of a narrator recounting the discourse of characters."*[11] Characters are, in effect, islands of consciousness over which the narrator has no control.

These limitations determine, in Ricoeur's view, the degree to which a narrative voice may be taken as a trustworthy source of meaning or significance. In works like *Pride and Prejudice* or *Middlemarch* or the later novels of Henry James, for instance, we view events through the eyes of a narrator who, in amplitude and complexity of moral consciousness, may surpass even the most fully conscious characters in the story. In such cases, the *totum simul* perspective from which the story is told is simply, as one might say, an advance version of the conclusions the more perceptive characters will themselves have drawn by the end of the story. The teleological movement of the story—that accelerating sense of pace as, say, Elizabeth and Darcy begin to comprehend each other—may thus be understood as a narrative version of something resembling magnetic attraction, with certain key characters being drawn ever more irresistibly toward the fixed position of a *totum simul* that, from the opening pages, has been occupied by a consciousness very like their own.

At the other extreme, we have the problem of the unreliable narrator, who occupies the *totum simul* position but who fails to understand the significance of events in the story. For Ricoeur, the importance of narrative unreliability is precisely that it shows that the *totum simul* is separate from the narrative point of view. The problem this poses is obvious. Since the narrator of a story—Gulliver in *Gulliver's Travels*, say, or John Dowell in Ford Madox Ford's *The Good Soldier*—is our sole source of information about what is occurring in the narrated world, and since we are nonetheless able to see in some cases that the narrator is prevaricating, or mistaken, or simply too obtuse to understand the significance of the details he has supplied, where is the notion of a "true" version of events coming from? A standard example in older college handbooks was Ring Lardner's "Haircut," in which a barber tells a customer the story of an accident that we understand, though he does not, to have been a murder. Exactly how, students were asked, can we know this when the narrator does not?

Ricoeur's answer is that in such cases the narrator, in missing the intrinsic significance of certain details in the story, vacates a point of view that may then be occupied by another consciousness within the text. Consider, for instance, *Gulliver's Travels*, in which the Gulliver who visits Lilliput, the land of tiny people—human beings, as he says, "less than six inches high"—is an indefatigable measurer, in standard units of inches, feet, and yards, of virtually everything he encounters: trees, buildings, gates, streets, city squares, and cultivated fields. His measurements are, if anything could be, what we should want to call intrinsic or objective facts. Yet when his enemies at court falsely accuse him of carrying on an illicit relationship with the Lord Treasurer's wife, Gulliver's defense introduces only the sort of evidence that any European courtier might use to defend himself: the lady never paid him a private visit, as his enemies have maliciously alleged. When she visited him it was "always publicly, nor ever without three more in the coach, who were usually her sister and young daughter, and some particular acquaintance." And so on.

Why does Gulliver not put forth the obvious defense that since the Lord Treasurer's wife is less than six inches tall, sex between the two of them is an anatomical impossibility? For Wayne Booth, on whose *Rhetoric of Fiction* Ricoeur to a certain degree draws, the answer famously lay in an "implied author who carries the reader with him in judging the narrator."[12] Yet where, since Gulliver's is the only voice we hear, and since his obsessive physical measuring supplies all the evidence one needs to grasp the irony, is the voice of this implied author coming from? To such narratologists as Seymour Chatman and Gérard Genette, Booth's "implied author" has seemed to amount to little more than an assertion that, since Gulliver is himself too obtuse to grasp the irony, we must posit an authorial consciousness whose ironic intention is constantly winking at us from the text. This may in some sense avoid the standard objection that the real Jonathan Swift, who is dead and buried in Dublin, cannot be the present source of irony. But it is hard to see how it means anything more than that *Gulliver's Travels* is ironic because it was written with an ironic intention.

Nonetheless, Ricoeur sees more in Booth's notion of the implied author than mere empty circularity. The reason is that the concept carries for him certain phenomenological implications missing from Booth's discussion. The most important takes us to the very core of Ricoeur's argument about time and narrative. It is that consciousness—not your consciousness, or mine, but consciousness in purely abstract terms, as a permanent and universal fact of human existence—must always be taken as the medium of literary comprehension. This is not a psychological proposition. Consider: you are now reading this sentence. In the ordinary sense, I know nothing about you—your age, your social circumstances, your location in time or geographical space—but I do know that if my words are, so to speak, coming alive in your mind at this moment, they are doing so in a consciousness like my own, and one subject to the same conditions of possibility for all human experience.

What, then, about Ricoeur's own understanding of the implied author? Again, consider: everything you know about the "I" that is now speaking to you comes from the words on the page. You may very well have no idea whether I am alive or dead—indeed, the hand that is now writing this sentence will have decomposed into dust by the time some readers come across these words—and what you have learned about me has come from a voice talking about specialized matters such as literary mimesis, the semantics of human action, and the like. But what is certain—we are close, now, to what Ricoeur will mean by "implied author"—is that you have been seeing or imagining or perceiving a consciousness behind the words, and a consciousness, moreover, not absolutely identical with or reducible to the words themselves. As Ricoeur himself might have put it, you have been listening to me not simply as a voice but as a person, not in exactly the same sense as the friend you might meet for lunch later today is a person, but not, at the same time, entirely different.

Ricoeur's term for the relation of the work to an actual human consciousness, and for what occurs when the work is taken up to be read, is "transcendence within immanence" ("transcendance immanente au texte").[13] What he means by immanence is clear enough. As I write this sentence, Tolkien's *Lord of the Rings* trilogy sits among other objects on the shelf across from me. But with this difference: the world of Middle Earth, of Frodo and Gandalf and Aragorn and the others, is "immanent" within its three volumes, waiting to be brought alive or set free in the consciousness of a reader, as is not the case with the pipe rack or tobacco jar sitting beside them on the same shelf. What Ricoeur means by "transcendence" then follows directly. As I begin to read, the world of Middle Earth takes shape as the setting of actions and events that are projected as having taken place independently of—that is, "transcending"—the narrative discourse in which they are reported. From a few paltry written marks on the page, as Vladimir Nabokov's Kinbote once says, there springs into existence a world.

So much is standard narratology, involving little more than the story-discourse distinction discussed in chapter 3. Ricoeur's originality lies in having seen that the principle of transcendence holds as well for the narrator, who, in perceiving the world of the story from a *totum simul* perspective, is projected as a unifying consciousness existing independently of the words on the page. It is the unity of this consciousness that is central to Ricoeur's conception. Thus, for instance, the narrator of *Tom Jones*, so chattily intrusive that he seems almost to become another character in the work, counts as an implied author. But so does the narrator of Woolf's *Mrs Dalloway*, although she is so completely absorbed into the story and its characters that little more than an abstract unity of consciousness remains. And so, at the farthest extreme, does the unseen editor or arranger of the correspondence in an epistolary novel like Richardson's *Clarissa*, whose unity is simply that of a consciousness that has been able to recognize a story *in* the materials that make up the text.

Given the notion of a wholly immanent narrative consciousness, the outlines of Ricoeur's total conception of narrative structure become clear. It is most easily visualized, perhaps, as a set of three concentric spheres, each involving what in phenomenological terms would be called a horizon of consciousness. At the center lies the consciousness of characters as volitional beings—Käte Hamburger's notion of characters as what we have heard Ricoeur call "centers of fictive consciousness"— operating in circumstances that stand independent of the narration.

This is the level at which fictional structure is most directly grounded in the semantics of action, at which choices are made, actions undertaken, and judgments continuously made or modified on the basis of interaction with others. Whenever a character speaks in a fictional work, as Hamburger puts it in *The Logic of Literature*, we are hearing a voice that comes directly out of its world, which to that extent exists within narrative structure as a self-contained sphere of motive and action.

At the same time, characters in the story only exist for us within the medium of the narrator's consciousness, which thus becomes within narrative structure a second, wider circumference that encloses their world. This is, for Ricoeur, the most important implication of the narrative preterite as discussed by Weinrich. The events of the story, to recall Ricoeur's phrase once more, always take place in the past of the narrative voice. We do, it is true, hear the voices of characters within the story as though they emanated directly from their own world, with no mediating narrative consciousness between us and them: "What is Mr. Darcy to me, pray, that I should be afraid of him?" Yet we are also to remember that what we are hearing for the first time, the narrator already knows. This is Mrs. Bennet, in short, as her utterance remains vivid in the consciousness of a narrator who not only knows the outcome of the story, but who has had time to look back over its events, to make judgments about its characters, and to ponder the meaning and significance of the whole.

The third and final sphere, enclosing the previous two, is that consciousness in which the story comes alive as a story, the activation of that transcendence within immanence we have discussed. This is the basis of the last major problem Ricoeur sets out to solve, which is what it means for fictive experience to have permitted actual readers to get outside their own sphere of mortal time. Ricoeur is wholly aware that one time-honored solution has been to declare that, properly considered, the world of the work is real, and that it is "real" readers whose world is transient, illusory, and subject to death and decay. This is not an absurd solution. *Pride and Prejudice* and *Mrs Dalloway* will, after all, be there to greet other readers centuries from now, when you and I are gone. This is the position taken by Gilbert, for instance, in Oscar Wilde's *The Critic as Artist*, describing Homer's *Iliad* as a world where

Helen still appears daily on the battlements to watch, on the plain below, the mighty struggle of warriors like Hector and Achilles: "Phantoms, are they? Heroes of mist and mountain? Shadows in a song? No: they are real. Action! What is action? It dies at the moment of its energy. . . . The world is made by the singer for the dreamer."[14]

Ricoeur's theory of the implied reader, which aims to take seriously the claims of literary autonomy without denying those of ordinary reality, is a response to such arguments. Though he borrows the term "implied reader" from Wolfgang Iser, he means, as in the case of Booth's "implied author," something rather different. The attraction of Iser's term for Ricoeur is that it is able to suggest an audience projected by the work itself. Consider, for instance, the narrator of Fielding's *Tom Jones* as he speaks directly to his readers, warning those to whom the novel is still an unfamiliar literary form to be prepared for an entirely new experience of fictive time:

> My reader then is not to be surprised, if, in the course of this work, he shall find some chapters very short, and others altogether as long; some that contain only the time of a single day, and others that comprise years. . . . for as I am, in reality, the founder of a new province of writing, so I am at liberty to make what laws I please therein. And these laws, my readers, whom I consider as my subjects, are bound to believe in and obey; with which that they may readily and chearfully comply, I do hereby assure them, that I shall principally regard their ease and advantage in all such institutions.[15]

When any actual reader takes up the *Tom Jones*, there arises a contest between opposing spheres of reality that Ricoeur will sometimes describe in terms of struggle or confrontation. He does not mean what Coleridge famously called the willing suspension of disbelief: the way the reader of Homer is called upon to believe that Achilles, say, having been dipped in a river by a goddess mother, could actually be invulnerable to ordinary wounds. What Ricoeur has in mind, rather, is the struggle involved when, in what might be called a depersonalization of consciousness, I adopt the point of view of the reader addressed in *Tom Jones*. For it is impossible that the narrator could be addressing some actual reader who, as it might be, lives in a United States with shopping malls and cell phones, or who has read scores of novels by authors not yet born, or who is able to compare *Tom Jones* with something called cinematic narrative, where stories are told by flickering images on a screen. He must specifically be understood as addressing a reader to whom the novel is a new literary form, but to whom, on the other hand, the eighteenth-century social world of Tom and Sophie and Squire Alworthy is otherwise entirely familiar.

This is, for Ricoeur, the spark that leaps over the ontological gap between fictional narrative and ordinary reality. In taking up the position of the implied reader of *Tom Jones*, I am also divesting my normal self of its particularities, leaving only a disembodied consciousness as the medium within which stories achieve what Ricoeur calls their transcendence within immanence. I have also entered a new world of fictive time, where narrative temporality mirrors a structure of meaning or significance born of human concern. The one thing I have not left behind, I discover, is a semantics of action wholly familiar to me from ordinary life. Tom and Sophie, as it turns out, as well as Blifel and Squire Western and the rest, dwell within the same realm of volition and motive and action as I and my friends and neighbors. Their understanding of their own existence is, like mine, rooted in what we have heard Ricoeur call the prenarrative structure of real action, the primordial stratum of social or communal consciousness that gives birth to narrative in every age and culture.

At the end of *Time and Narrative*, we find ourselves on ground familiar to us from its opening pages, a prenarrative understanding of the world—what we encountered, at the outset of our journey, as Mimesis$_1$—that at the level of everyday life generates the stories we tell to explain ourselves to others and others to ourselves. It is universal— if I were to meet a caveman, we would make ourselves understood to each other, if we managed to do so at all, through a shared grasp of such things as motives, choices, goals, and purposes—and has left as its finished monuments tales of the tribe, from the epic of Gilgamesh to Joyce's *Ulysses*. Its time, as Ricoeur has taught us, is not the cosmic time of a universe oblivious to human existence, nor yet the time of an isolated consciousness that, as Walter Pater once said, keeps as a solitary prisoner its dream of the world. It is a third time of narrative that, belonging to narrative alone, alone gives back the image of a world of human concern. It is, Ricoeur thinks, the time in which humanity has been dwelling, as unconsciously as it breathes the air, since its appearance on the face of the earth.

PAUL RICOEUR

A Philosophical Journey

THE FOLLOWING INTERVIEW IS TAKEN FROM A SPECIAL ISSUE of *Magazine littéraire* (September 2000) devoted to the work of Paul Ricoeur at just the moment that he was belatedly being recognized in his own country as a major French thinker of the twentieth century. Although the story of Ricoeur's rediscovery by younger French intellectuals can be glimpsed in the interview itself, a brief sketch may be useful in setting its context. Paul Ricoeur's earliest work was done as a member of the *Esprit* group founded in the 1930s by Emmanuel Mounier, a Catholic intellectual whose philosophy of "personalism" was an attempt to assert individual dignity as a core value in a Europe driven close to despair by economic depression and increasingly polarized by the attractions of Marxist doctrine and Communist party politics, on the one hand, and, on the other, by the glittering show of fascist power in Mussolini's Italy and Hitler's Germany.

When France fell to German forces in 1940 after a few weeks of fighting, Ricoeur was taken prisoner with his military unit. The story of his imprisonment is one of extraordinary mental concentration: living in overcrowded conditions, with insufficient heat and clothing, and subsisting on meager rations, he embarked on a systematic study of the German existentialist Karl Jaspers and of Edmund Husserl's *Ideen I*, a book that had not yet been translated into French. His translation of

Husserl, written in minute handwriting on the margins of the German edition—prisoners were forbidden to have writing paper—would play a vital part in Ricoeur's postwar emergence as one of the major figures in European phenomenology.

After the war, Ricoeur became an immensely influential teacher of philosophy at the Sorbonne, where his classes on Husserl and phenomenology, as well as on such canonical figures as Aristotle and Kant, drew so many students that loudspeakers had to be set up in the courtyard outside the lecture hall for the benefit of those unable to find seats. In 1967, having been a longtime advocate of major university reform, Ricoeur gave up his post at the Sorbonne to become *doyen*—literally "dean," but in American university terms closer to "provost" or "chancellor"—of the newly founded university of Nanterre.

The episode precipitating Ricoeur's disappearance from the Parisian intellectual scene came in May 1968, when explosive student protests plunged the French university system into turmoil. As both a Christian socialist and a prominent spokesman for university reform, Ricoeur found himself in sympathy with student demands. As *doyen*, he tried hard to bring about a genuine dialogue between the Ministry of Education and students of various left-wing groups. Nonetheless, when he failed to declare unconditional support for escalating "radical" demands, Ricoeur was denounced as a reactionary by students on the self-declared Maoist fringe. In succeeding days, when the French government called in the police, a bloody confrontation took place on the Nanterre university grounds. Ricoeur, dismayed by what he considered the extreme bad faith shown by both government and students, resigned his post.

With this act, he embarked on what would amount to a voluntary fifteen-year exile from Parisian intellectual life, during which he would become, paradoxically, one of the best-known philosophers in the English-speaking world. From 1970 onward, he held an endowed chair at the University of Chicago, from which he took occasional semester leaves to teach at the University of Louvain in Belgium. He made lecture tours as far afield as Japan. At the time I met him, at the National Humanities Center in 1979–80, Ricoeur was already highly regarded among my own generation of younger American scholars as the author of such works as *The Symbolism of Evil* and *Freud and Philosophy*. At that point, he had already made substantial progress on the project that would become *Temps et récit*, the first volume of which appeared in 1983, followed by an English translation the next year.

The importance of *Temps et récit* was immediately grasped by French intellectuals. The issue of *Magazine littéraire* from which the following interview has been translated contains a biographical essay on Ricoeur by François Dosse, whose *Paul Ricoeur: Les sens d'une vie* is so far the authoritative account of Ricoeur's life and work. When the first volume of *Temps et récit* appeared, reports Dosse, it was as though some brilliant and little-known philosopher from the French past had somehow been brought unexpectedly back to life. By the time the third volume appeared, it was as though a distant bell had sounded the hour of consecration: "an entire generation of younger intellectuals discovered with a sense of rapture the power and coherence of a thinker who had been steadily enriching his perspective without ceasing to bore ahead in a single direction through every obstacle. He became then for many of them the very model of the intellectual who remains engaged with present events while responding not as a 'master thinker' (*maître penseur*) but as someone who has mastered the art of thinking."

The interview was conducted by François Ewald on June 20, 2000, at Les Murs Blancs, a community founded by Emmanuel Mounier in 1939 for members of the *Esprit* group. Named for its high stone walls, which received regular coats of whitewash in the French rural manner, Les Murs Blancs was an abandoned estate south of Paris which had been reconstructed as a set of separate residences surrounded by communally owned parks and gardens. Paul Ricoeur and his wife Simone joined the community in 1956. After Simone's death in 1997, Ricoeur continued to live there for part of each year.

The occasion was the recent publication of Ricoeur's *La Memoire, l'histoire, l'oubli* (*Memory, History, Forgetting*). The interview catches Ricoeur at a moment when, having some time since made his peace with a Parisian intellectual scene from which he had once departed in great bitterness, he is able to look back over his career as an essentially completed whole. From that perspective, one sees that the controlling perspective of *Time and Narrative*—the notion of literary and historical works as enclosing worlds-in-themselves that nonetheless exist in the midst of, and may be incorporated into, the separate flow of mortal time—also lies at the center of Ricoeur's conception of philosophy. For philosophy, he says in his concluding exchange with François Ewald, also exists in that mysterious space of contemporaneity in which a dialogue with the dead may be carried on by living voices.

My translation of the *Magazine littéraire* interview was originally published in *Providence Studies in Western Civilization* (vol. 8, no. 2, Fall/Winter 2004). What follows is a shortened version meant to provide a context for, specifically, the exegesis of *Temps et récit* given in the foregoing chapters.

FRANÇOIS EWALD SETS THE SCENE:

At four o'clock in the afternoon on July 20, 2000, with the sky heavy with the threat of rain, we were welcomed by Paul Ricoeur into the calm stillness of "Mur blancs." We go up some steps and into a large, luminous room looking directly out onto the garden. For Magazine littéraire, *the philosopher retraces the itinerary leading to* La Mémoire, l'histoire, l'oubli.

—How should one describe the course of a career that begins in the 1950s with a thesis on the philosophy of the will and moves toward the important work you have just published, *Memory, History, and Forgetting*?

—I've never had a philosophy that you could call "my" philosophy, one that I'd push forward from one book to the next. Every one of my books was targeted at a specific problem. I've always thought in terms of problems. These are discontinuous.

I began my first work, on the philosophy of the will, as a disciple of Husserl. My approach was very close to that of Merleau-Ponty. He wanted to give an account of perception. I chose to work on a problem associated with the power to act, because I've always been preoccupied, no doubt due to my Protestant upbringing, with the flawed will, with the phenomena of blame and guilt. I began by asking myself what a free will could be: What was it free to do? What is it to will something? What is it to act on a body that might either passively obey or have urges of its own? What are the limits of the will? What part is played by involuntary thought or action? That first book—*The Voluntary and the Involuntary* (1950)—left a residual problem, one that I'd specifically set aside from consideration in the preface: the problem of evil.

My problem then was to try to understand how our perception of evil is structured, as well as how it has a power to impose structure on perception itself. I attempted to approach the problem through an examination of symbol and myth, which in a small way revolutionized the methods of pure description inspired by Husserl's phenomenology, which were those I was used to. I found myself confronted by numerous visions of the world in which the sense of evil was a major element: Greek tragedy, the biblical myth of Adam, the various Mesopotamian myths, and then everything culture has produced in the way of pseudo-myths or "rationalized myths" like the idea of Original Sin that begins with Augustine. That's how I lit upon the interpretive method that at the time seemed to me to be specifically related to symbolic discourse. Since the typology of the great myths of evil had a clear structure, I tried to lay out a sort of cartography of these visions. This came out as *The Symbolism of Evil* (1960).

This work, as before, left a residue or remainder, this time a Freudian one, which had tormented me from the beginning, namely, the whole problem of pathological culpability. I read Freud. For three years, I made Freud the focus of the course I was giving at the Sorbonne. This is how I came to think about the limits of consciousness, of the Unconscious, which had always been the point of failure for the phenomenological method which was my starting point.

—Your relations with Lacan and the Lacanians were difficult.

—It's so complicated that I still don't altogether understand what happened to me. Between me and Lacan there was some sort of cat-and-mouse game going on. He was the cat. Our relations began in Bonneval, where the accomplished psychiatrist Henry Ey had invited me to publicly expound my interpretation of Freud. Lacan was present. He returned to Paris with me. He tried to seduce me intellectually. He invited me to attend his seminar, which I did, without understanding a word.

At the same time, I continued to work on my book, which in fact had already taken shape, though not yet put into final form, during my teaching at the Sorbonne. When the book appeared—this was *Freud and Philosophy* (1965)—Lacan went crazy, in turn accusing me, and getting others to accuse me, either of plagiarism or of contempt.

—**That was the heyday of structuralism.**
—I was literally ostracized. It was only in the United States that I was able to go on talking about Freud, about psychoanalysis, about the way Freud had dealt with culture and the aesthetic. In France it was as though I had been placed under a sentence of banishment, in a way that was unjust, grotesque, and untrue. They said for instance that I had tried to incorporate psychoanalysis into the hermeneutic mode of interpretation, while in reality I had done just the reverse.

—**The work on Freud also left a residue or remainder?**
—Yes, the problem of what it means that there exist entirely different modes of interpretation. I had already encountered the same problem in literary criticism. I was able to carry on a friendly and productive argument with Julien Greimas.

We mutually esteemed each other. Our work was in some sense mutually implicated: I became a part of his semiotic analysis, he proceeded to give a semiotic analysis of my approach. We had each expanded our circle to enclose the other. It should be said that a third element entered our intellectual relation—analytic philosophy.

Analytic philosophy represented, for me, a constant imperative to strive not only for coherence but for a mastery of arguments bearing on any given point and for conceptual precision—all of which distanced me from the vague or systematically obscure mode of a Lacan or a Heidegger.

I had found myself brought up short by this style of clear argumentation, so different from that employed by the cult of literary gongorism, which at the same time forced me to come face to face with the problem of conflicting modes of interpretation. What is it to interpret something? This led me to the most fundamental questions about hermeneutics as such: What is meaning? What does it mean to understand something?

What exactly is a text? What is the relation between writing and reading? I also found myself confronted by three different branches of structuralism: the psychoanalytic branch represented by Lacan, the literary branch represented by Roland Barthes, and the branch of social science represented by Claude Lévi-Strauss, whose work I still consider to have monumental importance.

—We come now to your work on *The Conflict of Interpretations.*
—In earlier works, I'd skirted the possibility of relativism, and therefore of truth. To keep from being swallowed up in a morass of speculation, I sought for issues that would permit me to test the idea that there were a variety of interpretive modes. I immediately encountered two obvious themes: narrative and metaphor. In both cases, I'd have to deal with the same phenomenon, the production of new sense or new meanings that I call semantic innovation. It's possible to create meaning simply by telling a story. It's possible to create meaning by using a metaphor. The narrative and the poetic—I tried to go at these two large problems more or less simultaneously, starting with *The Rule of Metaphor* (1975), devoted to that fundamental means of producing sense that we call poetic language.

I rediscovered here something not very distant from a point made earlier by Heidegger, whom I'd been very carefully steering clear of, maybe to keep myself from being dazzled by his speculations. The point was this: to exist in the world by means of language is also necessarily to go on producing senses that go outside or beyond logic, beyond any meanings that could come simply from having a command over words. Language itself has certain deep creative powers which the Heideggerians would say are primitive or irreducible.

Having finished with metaphor, I turned to narrative, which includes an entire range of discourse that goes back to the earliest times. People have always told stories. We have here a widespread use of language, so popular and at the same time disclosing such deep connections to life, to other people, and to society as a whole that narrative is an inexhaustible treasure. And, quite apart from the play of language that makes it what it is, narrative is connected to time. My approach was to come at the problem of time not as the physicists or cosmologists do, but through the fact that we structure it. There is a way of taking up and separating off time that one may call "narrated time."

—Did *Time and Narrative* also leave a remainder or residue?
—The problem of memory. The residual problem left by *Time and Narrative* was its complete silence on memory and forgetting. So I once again confronted the whole problem of time. I had already tried to come at it through narrative. I needed now to come at it through memory, through our power to recognize or acknowledge what is remembered—through that whole moving spectacle in which memories vanish away into oblivion and yet may be brought back, as though we had been able permanently to reconquer some lost portion of the past through memory.

—In *La Mémoire, l'histoire, l'oubli* you situate yourself in relation to the great philosophers of the past. What is the major difference between your account of memory and those of Plato, Aristotle, or St. Augustine?
—My main contribution is to change the order in which the questions are asked. Take the question of memory. It's usual to begin by asking, due to the great and deserved influence of Augustine, how "I remember who I am and what happened to me." It's better to begin from a different question: "What is it to have a memory of something?" Here I was following the trail of classical Husserlian phenomenology: What is the *object* of our memories—not the consciousness that is doing the remembering but the thing or state of affairs of which someone who remembers is conscious? What is "a memory?" How is it different from a fantasy or illusion, or from an image?

This led to a second question: How does one seek or look for a memory? The Greeks, significantly, had two words for remembering: *mnémè*, or simple memory—I have a memory of something, a memory rises up spontaneously in my consciousness—and then *anamnésis*: I have to try or make an effort to remember. In that case: what is the relation between the feeling of longing associated with remembering and the actual effort to retrieve a memory?

This is where history enters, because history is the motor of such retrieval. And why? Precisely because history is never occupied with the *mnémè*, remembrance as it springs spontaneously into the mind. The historian searches endlessly for that lost object that Michel de Certeau has very justly called "the historical absent."

While a living memory has something immediate and unmistakable about it, history must construct, in the hope of reconstructing just this living quality. You might say that the deepest impulse of the historian lies not in writing but in *re*writing. When someone sets out to write a new book about the French Revolution, it's because they're not satisfied with the works that have been written so far. They wish to introduce something new, getting closer in their own account to something that seems to them essential. This movement toward a closer approximation of something lost or absent is the historian's counterpart of what happens when an individual sets out to recover a memory.

—**In taking up the subject of memory, one also necessarily takes up such matters as guilt or blame and responsibility.**

—No doubt, but these are concepts that have to be taken up in their proper order. My own thinking owes a great deal to a book on culpability written by Karl Jaspers in 1947, for which I'm filled with gratitude. He distinguishes between criminal culpability, which is always an individual matter to be taken up by the courts; political culpability, which has to do with those things for which, as someone who has enjoyed the benefits of a state or nation that has committed crimes, even though I've done nothing wrong myself, I am bound to make some sort of reparation; and moral culpability: what are those small acts of moral collapse or negligence which mean that I have in some sense contributed to crimes?

Then, finally, there's another concept of moral responsibility that I treat at the beginning of my latest book and which deals with the presence of a fundamental propensity to evil within human beings. This kind of responsibility lies outside the reach of judges or politicians or even moralists. It's an issue that can only be taken up through self-examination, alone or in the company of true friends. For me, this is the religious dimension of existence.

—The religious dimension that permits us to deal with moral responsibility is missing today?

—We have a need of grand symbols to give structure to that dark realm of human evil that lies beyond the reach of jurisprudence, politics, and even morality as such, what Kant had in mind in talking about a radical evil in opposition to an original goodness.

As radical as that evil may be, it is still less profound than the goodness that opposes it. However great the wickedness that one commits, there remains in every human being a core of goodness that can be brought out. That is why religion does not exist to condemn. It is a message that says: "You are worth more than your actions." The good that exists in everyone may be liberated only when they allow their lives to be structured by the grand symbols that lie at the foundation of the great religions.

—May we not say that we live in a society characterized by the disappearance of the symbolic?

—Certainly. This is the situation in which I see myself as pursuing my own work, hoping to help recover some of the ground that's been lost in the stripping away of the symbolic dimension. But I'm scarcely alone in this. Religions can hardly cover everything. They are only one of the forms of discourse available.

I deeply admire the formula that Simone Weil described as the four refusals or negations: "not to believe that anything is exempt from fate or chance, never to admire force that derives from mere power, never to hate your enemies, and never to humiliate those who suffer from misfortune." These are not simply negations or refusals, but principles that impose a certain moral structure on existence, a starting point from which we may go about inventing a positive form of life.

—Would this be one of the tasks of contemporary philosophy?

—The "contemporary" cannot be described. I have no coherent notion of the period during which I am alive. More importantly, I have no notion of my own place in history because I'm unable to imagine the viewpoint from which the historians of ages to come will look back at us.

—So you'd see your own philosophy as occupying a more atemporal position?

—Not atemporal, but transhistorical. All the books of the past lie open on my table. None is older than any other. A dialogue in Plato's work is still a dialogue in which I'm able to take part. Although it was written in ancient Greece, it hasn't been left behind by the flow of historical time as was, say, the economy of the ancient Greek city states. It may be lifted out of its historical context and given a new context in light of later problems and questions.

The classics are, for me and many others, the works that stand the test of time. They are always open to reading and rereading. I think of this as the space of a mysterious contemporaneity, in which what might be called a dialogue with the dead is nonetheless conducted by altogether living voices.

—You might want to say, in short, that philosophy is what survives the passage of time?

—It is its way of being eternal. Eternal not in the sense of being exempt from time, but in the sense of passing along the stream of time while maintaining the strong and ineradicable identity of its classic texts.

NOTES

Notes to the French original are cued, with volume and page number, as TR: Paul Ricoeur, *Temps et récit*, 3 vols. (Paris: Éditions de Seuil, 1983–85). Notes to the English translation are cued as TN: *Time and Narrative*, 3 vols., trans. Kathleen McLaughlin and David Pellauer (Chicago: University of Chicago Press, 1984–88).

Preface

1. François Dosse, *Paul Ricoeur: Les sens d'une vie* (Paris: Éditions de Découverte & Syros, 2001), 552.

CHAPTER 1 Mimesis

1. TN, 1:57.
2. Roland Barthes, "Introduction to the Structural Analysis of Narrative," in *The Semiotic Challenge*, trans. Richard Howard (New York: Hill and Wang, 1988), 95.
3. TR, 1:366.
4. Dickens, *A Tale of Two Cities* (New York: New American Library, 1964), 270–71.
5. Weinrich, as qtd. in TN, 2:71. Ricoeur in TR quotes from *Temps: Le récit et le commentaire* (Paris: Seuil, 1973), a French translation by Michèle Lacoste (with revisions) of Harald Weinrich, *Tempus: Besprochene und erzählte Welt* (Stuttgart: Kohlhammer, 1964).

6. Barthes, *The Semiotic Challenge*, 95.

7. Jonathan Culler, *In Pursuit of Signs* (Ithaca: Cornell University Press), 38.

8. David Parker, *The Self in Moral Space* (Ithaca: Cornell University Press, 2007), 8. Parker borrows the term from the work of Charles Taylor.

CHAPTER 2 Time

1. Augustine, *Confessions*, trans. R. S. Pine-Coffin (New York: Penguin Books, 1961), bk. 11, 14.17. Further quotations of Augustine on time are from this translation.

2. Immanuel Kant, *Critique of Pure Reason*, trans. Norman Kemp-Smith (London: MacMillan, 1933), A38/B54, p. 79. Further quotations of Kant are from this translation.

3. Ibid., A182/B226, p. 213.

4. From *Nature*, ch. 7 ("Spirit"), in *Ralph Waldo Emerson*, ed. Richard Poirier (Oxford: Oxford University Press, 1990), 30.

CHAPTER 3 Narrativity

1. Barthes, "Introduction to the Structural Analysis of Narrative," 95.

2. See Appendix, 109.

3. Foucault, *The Archaelogy of Knowledge*, trans. A. M. Sheridan Smith (New York: Pantheon, 1972), 13. (Translation altered. Original: "les recherches psychanalytiques, linguistiques, puis ethnologiques, on dépossède le sujet des lois de son désir, des formes de sa parole, des règles de son action." *L'Archeologie du savoir* [Paris: Gallimard, 1969], 22.)

4. Barthes, *The Semiotic Challenge*, 5.

5. Ibid., 98.

6. TN, 2:86. Italics in original.

7. Northrop Frye, *Anatomy of Criticism* (Princeton: Princeton University Press, 1957), 163.

8. Culler, *The Pursuit of Signs*, 171.

9. Jane Austen, *Pride and Prejudice* (London: Oxford University Press, 1962), 97.

10. TN, 1:80; TR, 1:151.

11. Qtd. in Myra Jehlen, *Five Fictions in Search of Truth* (Princeton: Princeton University Press, 2009), 3.

CHAPTER 4 Semantics of Action

1. TN, 1:180.

2. Charles Frankel, "Explanation and Interpretation in History," in *Theories of History*, ed. Patrick Gardiner (New York: The Free Press, 1959), 410. Qtd. in TN, 1:115.

3. TN, 1:129.

4. W. H. Dray, *Laws and Explanations in History* (London: Oxford University Press, 1957), 121, italics in original. Qtd. in TN, 1:129.

5. Ibid., 132. Qtd. in TN, 1:130.

6. TN, 1:131.

7. Ricoeur's English translators use the term "interference." I shall retain Ricoeur's vocabulary.

8. H. G. von Wright, *Explanation and Understanding* (Ithaca: Cornell University Press, 1971), 60, italics in original. Qtd. in TN, 1:135.

9. My formulation, based on TN, 1:136.

CHAPTER 5 Poetics of History

1. W. B. Gallie, *Philosophy and the Historical Understanding* (New York: Schocken Books, 1968), 23. Qtd. in TN, 1:150.

2. TN, 1:101.

3. Louis O. Mink, "Philosophical Analysis and Historical Understanding," *Review of Metaphysics* 20 (1968): 687. Qtd. in TN, 1:157.

4. TN, 1:208; TR, 1:365.

5. Foucault, *Archaeology of Knowledge*, 3.

CHAPTER 6 Poetics of Fiction

1. TN, 2:77; TR, 2:54.

2. Dickens, *Tale of Two Cities*, 215.

3. Quotations are from Virginia Woolf, *Mrs Dalloway*, ed. Claire Tomalin (Oxford: Oxford University Press, 1992); Thomas Mann, *The Magic Mountain*, trans. H. T. Lowe-Porter (New York: Alfred A. Knopf, 1972; Vintage Books, 1969); Marcel Proust, *Remembrance of Things Past*, trans. C. K. Scott Moncrieff, Terence Kilmartin, and Andreas Mayor, 3 vols. (New York: Random House, 1981).

4. TN, 2:114.

5. TR, 2:252.

6. Proust, as qtd. in TN, 2:142.

7. Ibid., TN, 2:150.

8. Ibid., TN, 2:146.

9. Beneveniste, as qtd. in TN, 2:64.

10. TN, 2:89; TR, 2:167.

11. TN, 2:88. Italics in original.

12. Wayne Booth, *The Rhetoric of Fiction* (Chicago: University of Chicago Press, 1961), 158.

13. TR, 2:109.

14. Oscar Wilde, "The Critic as Artist," in *Oscar Wilde: The Major Works*, ed. Isobel Murray (Oxford University Press, 1989), 258–59.

15. Henry Fielding, *Tom Jones* (London: Penguin, 1985), 88 (bk. 2, ch. 1).

INDEX

actants, 42, 50, 79
Adorno, Theodor, 72
anagnorisis, 9, 10, 15, 51; and double temporality, 49; as convergence of *telos* and *totum simul*, 88
analytic philosophy, 108
anamnésis: defined, 110
Annales history, 83–84
Aristotle, 22, 31, 51, 52, 68; *Physics*, 20–21, 69, 75, 86; *Poetics*, xii, 1, 2, 4–5, 7–8, 13, 15, 41, 46
Aron, Raymond, 59, 81
Augustine, 19–21, 24–25, 27, 34, 69, 86; on Original Sin, 107
Austin, J. L., x

Barthes, Roland, 7, 13, 37, 39, 86, 109
basic action: defined, 63
Beardsley, Monroe, xi
Benveniste, Émile, 14, 93
Bloch, Marc, 82
Boethius, 9
Booth, Wayne, 95, 96
Braudel, Fernand, 53, 82–84
Bremond, Claude, 43–45
Brower, Reuben, xi

Carlyle, Thomas, 85–87
catharsis, 51
Certeau, Michel de, 111
characters: as centers of fictive consciousness, 93
Chatman, Seymour, 95
Chomsky, Noam, 37
Cohn, Dorrit, 93
Coleridge, Samuel Taylor, 99
Collingwood, R. G., 56–58, 60, 81
concordia discors, 6
consciousness: as medium of literary comprehension, 96, 100
Copernicus, 16
counterfactual inference, 59
covering law model, 57–59
Culler, Jonathan, 14, 47

Danto, Arthur, xii, 63, 77
Dickens, Charles: *A Tale of Two Cities*, 11–13, 46, 85, 87
diegetic narrative, 10, 46
Dilthey, Wilhelm, 55, 61, 66, 76
distentio animi, 25
Dosse, François, ix, 105
double temporality, 48–49; in historical writing, 83

119

WILLIAM C. DOWLING

is University Distinguished Professor of English at Rutgers University.

In literary theory, he is the author of *Jameson, Althusser, Marx:*

An Introduction to "The Political Unconscious" and *The Senses of the Text:*

Intensional Semantics and Literary Theory.

W. C. Dowling and Paul Ricoeur,
National Humanities Center, 1980.
Photograph by Kent Mullikin.